Days of MAJESTY

❧ Days of ❧
MAJESTY

SIMON WELFARE & ALASTAIR BRUCE

CROSS RIVER PRESS
A Division of Abbeville Publishing Group
New York   London   Paris

First published in the United States of America in 1993 by
Cross River Press, a division of Abbeville Publishing Group,
488 Madison Avenue, New York, NY 10022.

First published in Great Britain in 1993 by
Michael O'Mara Books Limited,
9 Lion Yard, Tremadoc Road, London SW4 7NQ.

ISBN 1-55859-657-7

Designed by Martin Bristow
Picture Research by Ava-Lee Tanner
Typeset by Florencetype Limited, Kewstoke, Avon

THIS BOOK IS FOR OUR FRIENDS WHO CREATED THE TELEVISION DOCUMENTARY
ON WHICH IT IS BASED: JOHN, PETER, HELEN, PHILIPPA, AVA-LEE, ANNE, MAGGIE,
CLAIRE, CAROLINE AND NEIL

HALF-TITLE: *The Queen leaves Buckingham Palace for her Coronation at Westminster Abbey in the
Gold State Coach drawn by eight Windsor Greys*

FRONTISPIECE: *Prince Philip pays homage to the newly crowned Queen in Westminster Abbey*

OPPOSITE: *Members of the Yeomen of the Guard at Royal Maundy*

CONTENTS

OPENING CEREMONIES

There are some curious subjects which have become old-fashioned – which have drifted, by degrees, so far outside the necessities of ordinary educations and occupations, that most of us grow up and live and die with but a faint perception that they exist at all, and with the incompletest notion of their details. If accident should bring any of them under our observation, we look at them with more or less indifference, according to our particular proclivities; but, as we get on very well without them, as they have nothing to do with money-making, or athletic sports, or Ritualism, or novels, or last night's ball, or the state of the crops, or the few remaining topics which now possess the privilege of interesting one or other of our social strata, we never think of going out of our way to make an explanation of them. And yet, however superannuated they may be, they are seldom altogether stupid: they all contain some sort of teaching; they may even occasionally be enlivening . . .

FREDERIC MARSHALL *International Vanities* 1875

The official Coronation portrait of the Queen taken in 1953 by the society photographer Cecil Beaton. In her left hand, she holds the Orb. Designed for the coronation of Charles II, it is decorated with more than 700 jewels, including 365 diamonds and 375 pearls. In her right hand, the Queen holds the Sceptre of Kingly Power and Mercy. Set into its head is the largest cut diamond in the world, Cullinan I. She is wearing the Imperial State Crown, which contains Edward the Confessor's sapphire.

TRUE to an age-old tradition, the weather was the main talking-point in Britain on Coronation Day, 1953. It virtually eclipsed the splendour of the ancient rites in which the young queen, Elizabeth II, was crowned and the news that Everest, the world's highest mountain, had at last been climbed by a British-led team.

Yet the date, 2 June, had been chosen with the utmost care. June, after all, marked High Summer in England. Fine weather, therefore, was almost guaranteed: warmth for happy crowds to bask in on the streets of London, sunshine to burnish the gold, silver and diamonds brought out to celebrate the dawning of the new Elizabethan Age.

But 2 June 1953 turned out quite differently. Snow lay on the summits of the Pennine Hills of northern England, the crowds shivered in temperatures typical of a day in January, drizzle soaked proud uniforms and bedraggled flags, street parties and country celebrations were rained off throughout the land.

However, few other things went awry on the day: many spectators collapsed with exhaustion, six soldiers were treated for accidental bayonet wounds sustained during the processions, some unfortunates slipped on rain-soaked roads and pavements, and the Prime Minister, Sir Winston Churchill, lost his place in the procession when his carriage broke down.

Unruffled, in a broadcast late that evening, the old leader found words that captured the feelings of a jubilant nation. 'We have had a day which the

oldest are proud to have lived to see and which the youngest will remember all their lives,' he said. Churchill also knew that behind the unforgettable colour and pageantry lay an extraordinary feat of organization.

Fourteen months had barely proved time enough. But by midnight on 1 June, when the roads in central London were closed to all but essential traffic, everything was in place. Some 1,740 yards of gold rope, tassels, braid and embroidered cloth festooned the furnishings in Westminster Abbey, and 2,287 yards of carpet covered its floor. There were 3,280 special telephone lines, routed through a special Coronation Exchange, standing by for the Press. And 29,200 troops from all over Britain and the Commonwealth were preparing to march in the procession or line its route. Sightseers had reached London in more than 6,000 coaches and as many extra trains. A staggering 30,000 caterers were waiting to feed them from kitchens set up in the Royal Parks and behind the viewing stands. Eleven acres of flowers had been specially grown and cut. Every last detail had been attended to: according to the official record, the 23 female lavatory attendants on duty in the Abbey were 'dressed in white overalls with the Royal Cypher EIIR embroidered on each lapel (and were given the opportunity afterwards of purchasing these at £1 each.)'

Few people slept that night in a capital city bright with bunting. Those without tickets to the stands took what rest they could on the pavements where they planned to spend the next day. Watching journalists noted that even in Buckingham Palace the lights came on well before five o'clock.

Four men had been given the task of organizing this great pageant. Along with his title, the Duke of Norfolk had inherited the ancient office of Earl Marshal of England. This made him the nation's 'Master of Ceremonies', responsible to the Crown for the most solemn state occasions, particularly royal funerals and coronations. In charge of the huge programme of public works surrounding the events in 1953 was a politician, David Eccles, the

Minister of Works. Two others held sway inside Westminster Abbey itself: the Archbishop of Canterbury, Dr Geoffrey Fisher, and the Honourable Sir George Rothe Bellew, Garter King of Arms. For centuries, Garter's duties have included helping the Earl Marshal to orchestrate the great royal ceremonies of England.

Late on the night before the Coronation, Sir George decided to make one last check on all his arrangements. The lights were low as he made his way through the Abbey. 'It was completely empty and dead,' he recalls, 'dead quiet.' Or so he thought.

As I approached the altar, I, of course, came into view of St Edward's Chair, which the Queen is actually crowned on. I expected to find it empty but to my surprise it was occupied. Heavens alive, on a night like this, to find St Edward's Chair, the most venerable chair in the world probably, occupied by two individuals – or rather one sitting in it and one standing by, loafing around! They were two women, two dear old bodies, typical old cleaning ladies from the Ministry of Works having a final brush-up, I suppose, and taking a little time off to have a natter. I'd thought they were ghosts or something from the past. It was a very, very frightening moment. I didn't say anything to them. I just left them there. But on the way out I told the police that they might perhaps be asked to enjoy a natter in some less sacred place.

The day held few other surprises, for Sir George had left little to chance. Every stage of the service was precisely timed: the Queen's walk up the

Westminster Abbey prepared for the Coronation. This area of the Abbey, in which the most solemn rituals of the ceremony take place, is known as the 'theatre'. The five-stepped platform was originally designed to raise the new monarch above his subjects. In 1953, its dimensions, laid down in medieval manuscripts, were faithfully reproduced by the Ministry of Works builders.

Abbey had been paced out by Lady Bellew in the garden of their home. The outline of the nave had been laid out on the lawn and she wore an old curtain to simulate the Sovereign's train. Two tiny gold stars had been stuck onto the velvet cap in the St Edward's Crown to ensure that the Archbishop of Canterbury placed it on the Queen's head the right way round. This worked well although the omens had not been good. A similar trick had been tried at the coronation of George VI, but the marker of red thread had disappeared, no doubt at the hands of some tidy-minded busybody, and the Archbishop was left to guess the correct orientation. George VI recorded in his diary:

I had taken every precaution as I thought to see that the crown was put on the right way round, but the Dean and the Archbishop had been juggling with it so much that I never did know whether it was right or not . . . the crown of England, weighs seven pounds, and it had to fit.

It is said that ever afterwards the King maintained that he had been crowned backwards. In 1953, Sir George had even sent an emissary with a stopwatch to check how long it took for the Archbishop to say prayers.

The hard work paid off. Everything went like clockwork inside the Abbey: the service began two minutes early but ended just one minute late.

Just before his death in 1992, another veteran of Coronation Day 1953, Company Sergeant Major Fred Clutton of the King's Company, Grenadier Guards, remembered the breath-taking beauty of the scene conjured up in Westminster Abbey by Sir George and his colleagues:

On the night before the Coronation, London was one huge campsite. Crowds arrived a day early to secure a good view of the processions and spent a cold, wet night on the pavement.

ABOVE: *The Coronation, or St Edward's, Chair in which the Queen was crowned. In 1953, scientific investigations revealed that it had had at least seven coats of paint since its construction in 1300 by Edward I's top craftsman, Walter the Painter. The Chair holds the Stone of Scone, or Stone of Destiny, on which the Kings of Scotland were traditionally crowned. This was stolen by Scottish protestors in 1951, but was recovered and restored to the Chair in time for the Coronation.*

RIGHT: *'Morning After'. Cartoonist David Low caused controversy by criticizing expenditure on the Coronation. In fact, much of the outlay was recovered from the sale of guests' chairs and the material used in the public works.*

It was a vision of Heaven. The great church was aglow with candles and television lights, with the rich hues of newly woven carpets and banners, with the glint of jewels and coronets. The air was filled with the rustle of scarlet robes and the scent of flowers. Music soared to the vaulted roof.

Two sociologists described the atmosphere outside:

The extraordinary stillness and tranquillity of the people on the route all through the early morning of 2 June was noted by many who moved among them . . . It was the same type of atmosphere, except that it was more pronounced, that one notices at Christmas-time when, in busy streets and crowded trains, people are much more warm-hearted, sympathetic and kindly than they are on more ordinary occasions. . . . Antagonism emerged only against people who did not seem to be joining in the great event or treating with proper respect the important social values – by failing, for example, to decorate their buildings with proper splendour. A minor example of the increase in communal unity was the police report that, contrary to their expectations, the pickpockets, usually an inevitable concomitant of any large crowd, were entirely inactive during Coronation Day.

Predictably a few voices of dissent were raised against this 'great nation-wide communion', most strikingly that of the cartoonist David Low who created outrage in some circles by lampooning the event as a multi-million-pound binge. But for most people, 2 June 1953 was a day on which feuds were forgotten, enemies danced together in the streets, and the red, white and blue of hats, rosettes and ribbons banished the bleakness of the post-war world.

The two sociologists mentioned above visited some of the boisterous street parties of the East End of London in search of material for a learned paper on *The Meaning Of The Coronation* and were amazed to note that most of the jolly folk enjoying the knees-up cared little for, and knew less about, the significance of the ceremony taking place a few miles away at

Celebrations in Morpeth Street in the East End of London. Street parties like this were held throughout Britain on Coronation Day. Communities spent weeks beforehand raising money: Morpeth Street's 'knees-up' cost £163. The children were usually given souvenirs. Coronation mugs were the most popular, but sets of red, white and blue pencils and crown-shaped paintboxes were also handed out.

Westminster. 'Nothing was more remarkable than the complete inability of people to say why they thought important the occasion they were honouring with such elaborate ritual,' they noted sniffily.

In fact, the roots of the ceremony are very ancient. Almost a thousand years have passed since William the Conqueror was crowned at Westminster Abbey in London on Christmas Day 1066. And, with only two exceptions, all the kings and queens of England who succeeded him have ridden or walked in procession to their coronations at the church which originally stood amid the marshes of the Isle of Thorns in the River Thames. Built by Edward the Confessor to excuse himself from a pilgrimage to Rome, it was rebuilt by Henry III and designed specifically for coronations, the most sacred ceremony of the realm.

Many of the rites performed at William's coronation date back to much earlier times: to 973AD when Edgar the Peaceable was crowned at Bath and even farther back to the days of the Germanic tribes. Their kings had to prove their entitlement to the throne by successfully balancing upon the upraised shields of their knights. This was by no means the easiest of ceremonies to perform and several aspiring monarchs almost forfeited their throne, notably Gumbald, King of Burgundy, who tottered dangerously while being hefted into the air by over-zealous followers. An echo of this could still be heard in 1953 when the Queen was 'lifted' into the Chair of Estate to claim her kingdom.

The basic order of service still followed at the coronation service is a little more modern. It is contained in a richly illuminated book called *Liber Regalis* now kept in the library of Westminster Abbey. When there is a monarch to be buried and a coronation to organize, its pages are still urgently consulted by the Earl Marshal and the Church authorities. Yet the ritual in *Liber Regalis* was already long-established when it was written after the crowning of Richard II in the late fourteenth century. It is said that if a medieval king had magically been transported through time to the Coronation of Queen Elizabeth II, he would have seen a coronation service almost indistinguishable from his own. Conversely, a film of the ceremony in 1953 is currently used as a teaching-aid by a London University lecturer in her course on the history of the Middle Ages.

A page from Liber Regalis, *the medieval 'handbook' still used in the planning of modern coronations. This manuscript, written at the end of the fourteenth century, is the fourth revision of an order of service drawn up more than a thousand years ago.*

As far as ceremonial is concerned, the high seriousness with which Queen Elizabeth approached her Coronation set the tone for her reign. With the help of Archbishop Fisher, she prepared for the religious rites by making a careful study of the liturgy and in the days before the service she rehearsed the complicated moves repeatedly both in the Abbey and at Buckingham Palace. Forty years later, she is said to be concerned that repeated showings of the moment of her crowning on television will devalue the solemnity of the greatest and most sacred royal ceremony of all.

Since then, day in and day out, the Court Circular, published in the newspapers, has chronicled the staging of ceremonies both large and small, public and private. The Queen's courtiers have often proved adept at altering and modernizing ceremonial to suit changing circumstances. For example, the need to forge a warmer, more approachable relationship with her people led to the creation of the popular royal 'walkabout,' while the investiture of Prince Charles as Prince of Wales in 1969 was held under a transparent canopy to provide a good view for the television cameras and the armchair audience.

In some cases, the public appetite for pomp and circumstance has been played upon, especially if the cause of enhancing the mystique of the monarchy could also advanced. A striking example of the 'antiquing' of ceremonial occurred in 1953 when the Royal Mews found that it had too few carriages for the Coronation procession. They were rescued by Sir Alexander Korda, proprietor of a major film studio, who provided four from the props department. Among the dignitaries they bore was the indomitable Queen Salote of Tonga whose refusal to shelter from the rain delighted the crowds. Thus was the fairy-tale image of royalty preserved.

A well-timed ceremony can also boost morale. While there is a long tradition of celebrating silver jubilees, the Queen's in 1977 is thought by one leading historian to have been primarily designed, in a changing world, 'as a perfect tonic to Britain's declining self-esteem'.

The Queen's father, King George VI, had similar good intentions when he revived and redesigned the ceremonies of the Order of the Garter after World War II. He thought there had never been a greater need for the nation to take refuge from the struggles of building the new world order in harking back to the heady days of chivalry and romance that the Order stands for.

Less noble motives have lain behind other innovations in the twentieth century. For example, the investiture of the Prince of Wales, later Edward VIII, at Caernarvon in 1911 was an invented ceremony which owed more to the political ambitions of David Lloyd-George than to history or

The investiture of Prince Charles as Prince of Wales in July 1969. The ceremony was organized by his uncle Lord Snowdon, and theatrical designer Carl Toms provided a dramatic contemporary setting: a circle of Welsh slate beneath a canopy. This was transparent to allow the television cameras to record the event unhindered.

constitutional necessity. In fact, the last investiture had taken place three hundred years before and the ritual had to be cobbled together. The presentation of the prince to the people on the castle battlements was a popular success, but the prince himself found it all rather hard to take, particularly the 'knights-of-old' cut of his costume. 'What will my Navy friends say if they see me in this preposterous rig?' he complained.

That same year saw one of the most spectacular pageants of the twentieth century, the Delhi Durbar. Here, an Indian tradition was pressed into the service of the British Empire. The idea behind it was blatant: amid great splendour the King-Emperor, George V, would demonstrate his imperial power to the Indian people and their local rulers.

'It would tend to allay unrest,' he wrote, 'and, I am sorry to say, seditious spirit, which unfortunately exists in some parts of India.' Garrard, the Crown Jeweller, was called in to run up a special Indian Crown; Sir Edward Elgar composed a fine tune. A city for 40,000 was erected on the outskirts of Delhi, railway lines and camp stations were constructed, 90,000 rats were put to death. The King and Queen stood under a canopy in their coronation robes to receive the homage of a seemingly never-ending line of rajahs.

The 1911 Durbar was the last of its kind, for the end of Empire in India made such shows of pomp and circumstance redundant. Nevertheless, the London *Times* reported that the Durbar had achieved its purpose:

Enthroned on high beneath a golden dome, looking outwards to the far north whence they came, their Majesties the King-Emperor and Queen-Empress were acclaimed by over 100,000 of their subjects. The ceremony at its culminating point exactly typified the Oriental conception of the ultimate repositories of Imperial power. The Monarchs sat alone, remote, but beneficent, raised far above the multitude, but visible to all, clad in rich vestments, flanked by radiant emblems of authority, guarded by a glittering array of troops, the cynosure of the proudest Princes of India, the central figures in what was surely the most majestic assemblage ever seen in the East.

Events of far less magnitude than the end of Empire also leave indelible marks upon ceremonies. When a rotten spar on the gun carriage broke at Queen Victoria's funeral in 1901, the horses were replaced by sailors plucked from the troops lining the streets. The idea proved popular and a naval contingent has pulled the monarch's coffin on its gun-carriage ever since.

The chaos of the day had another, more important consequence. It led to a tightening-up of the organization behind royal ceremonies. This, in its turn, established Britain's reputation as the last bastion of impeccably produced pomp and circumstance. 'Ceremony,' old courtiers are wont to muse, 'is what Britain does best.'

Yet is this the only reason why ceremonial has survived and, indeed, flourishes, in the last years of the twentieth century? The tourists who gather outside Buckingham Palace every morning to watch the Changing of the Guard bear witness to the enduring appeal of pageantry, meticulously executed to the music of a military band. Or have royal ceremonies been retained as morale-boosters, to be called upon whenever national spirits flag, providing, in another of Churchill's memorable phrases, 'a flash of colour on the hard road we have to travel?'

Shakespeare recognized that monarchs used ceremonial to assert power over their subjects, creating 'awe and fear in other men'. But does this still hold true in a less deferential age in which monarchs counsel, encourage and warn rather than rule with an iron fist? Or has ceremonial survived because it is still essential to the relationship between the Sovereign and the outside world? Some observers believe that it is through ceremonial that the Queen can best conduct business with her subjects, her Church, her armed forces, her country's institutions, politicians, foreign governments and even members of her own family. At the same time she remains a mystical figure, set apart and ordained by God through the supreme ceremony of her Coronation.

Finally, should royal ceremonies be allowed to survive even longer – into the twenty-first century and beyond?

Two tales of a couple of memorable years for royal ceremonies, may lead us to some of the answers. In 1952, the British people were preparing for a Coronation; in 1992, they were celebrating the fortieth anniversary of the Queen's accession to the throne.

Both stories, described in the next section, begin on the green acres of London's Hyde Park. The drumming of horses' hooves and the rattle of field-guns fill the cold air of a February morning. The King's Troop of the Royal Horse Artillery is approaching . . .

Imperial splendour: George V and Queen Mary at the Delhi Durbar in 1911. The event was a spectacular but curious mixture of traditions from East and West. The King even appointed a Delhi Herald to help in its organization.

THE CEREMONIES OF SPRING

Power is like the wind: we cannot see it, but we feel its force. Ceremonial is like the snow: an insubstantial pageant, soon melted into thin air.

DAVID CANNADINE *Rituals of Royalty* 1987

February

Each year of royal ceremonies begins in February in London's Hyde Park with the colour, smoke and thunder of a 41-gun salute.

In 1992, the shots that rang out at noon on 6 February were fired in celebration: 40 years earlier, on this day, Elizabeth II had become Queen.

The tradition of gun salutes goes back so far that its origins are lost. It is probably as old as artillery itself. All that is known for certain is that in the fifteenth century no celebration was complete without an exuberant discharge of shot. Two hundred years later, gun salutes marked all important anniversaries, such as the overthrow of the Gunpowder Plot in 1605: it is thought that this gave birth to the tradition of letting off fireworks on 5 November.

The reason for the number of shots fired is also obscure. For the past three hundred years, all gun salutes have been of odd numbers. For example, 13

LEFT: *Princess Elizabeth and her father King George VI in 1942. The King passed on his love of ceremony to his daughter.*

RIGHT: *The King's Troop of the Royal Horse Artillery fire a gun salute in Hyde Park, London. The Troop was given its name by George VI in 1947 and, at the Queen's request, retained it in his memory after her accession to the throne.*

shots were fired to celebrate St George's Day in 1670 and 61 guns on 5 November in 1683. Some experts suggest that this stems from a belief in the magical properties of uneven numbers noted by Shakespeare in *The Merry Wives of Windsor*: 'They say that there is divinity in odde numbers . . . I hope good luck lies in odde numbers.' Others argue that the answer lies in the way salutes used to be fired from ships. Gun decks always had an even number of cannons, but it was often impossible to see the signal to fire from there. So the gun on the poop deck cued the broadside guns, thus making an odd number of shots.

Despite this long tradition, Commanding Officers of the King's Troop like Major M.C.R. Wallace have found the Accession Salute an ordeal:

However much the Troop practises this Salute (generally two or three times) there is always a risk, as with most of the Troop's parades, that something can go wrong. If the mechanics of a Salute are examined, it can easily be seen what enormous scope for error exists. Seventy-one horses and 53 men come into line at the north end of the Park and then gallop across the grass and zig-zagging paths to the Saluting Base; 36 of these horses, divided into six teams, have a ton-and-a-half of gun and limber behind them. On arrival, the 'detachments' or men who fire the gun must dismount at the canter and bring the piece 'into action' in double quick time, while the limbers and 'empty horses' return to the 'wagon lines' as fast as they came. Twenty-three horses in all require to be led on the return journey. A sigh of relief can be heard all round as the first one-pound charge detonates on the dot of noon

In February 1952, the 56-gun salute, one for each year of his life, was one of the first public ceremonies to mark the King's death. High in The Round Tower of Windsor Castle, a little-known bell sounded out its solitary salute.

February 1952: A detachment from the Honourable Artillery Company, the oldest regiment in the British Army, marks the death of King George VI with a gun salute from the Tower of London. The guns had been used as artillery during the Second World War.

Only tolled at the passing of a Sovereign, the Sebastopol Bell, was captured during the Crimean War in 1855 and given to Queen Victoria.

In private, the ancient process of securing the succession was underway. In many countries in the past this has proved a ticklish business. French kings continued to rule even after their deaths until their successor had been crowned. This led to grisly scenes of courtiers propping up the royal corpse and pretending to ply it with food until the coronation had taken place.

In Britain, although the closest relation of the newly dead monarch always has first claim to the throne, succession is not automatic. The heir apparent has to apply to the Accession Council for permission to ascend the throne. The Council dates back more than a thousand years to the days of the Anglo-Saxon kings. Their reigns were invariably short and their deaths usually violent. As a result, the line of succession was by no means obvious. For example, in Wessex, not one son followed his father onto the throne between 685 and 839. The saga of the kings of Mercia, quoted by the constitutional historian W. Stubbs, is typical:

In Mercia, after Penda, his sons Wulfhere and Ethelred reigned in succession. Ethelred was followed by his nephew Cenred son of Wulfhere; Cenred by Ceolred son of Ethelred. Ethelbald the next king was a distant kinsman, great-nephew of Penda; Beornred who followed was a usurper. Offa recovered the throne for the royal house, but himself was only sprung from a brother of Penda. His son Egfrith succeeded him; on Egfrith's death Coenwulf, a distant collateral came in; his brother Ceolwulf succeeded after the murder of the child Kenelm; and the rest of the Mercian kings are not within the pedigree.

The Anglo-Saxon Witan, a council of clergy and nobles, was expected, if not to make sense of all this, then at least to endorse the most plausible claimant. Despite the replacement of the Witan by the Privy Council and Parliament, the tradition lives on in the form of the Accession Council. Its membership is made up of 'the Lords Spiritual and Temporal of the Realm assisted by the members of his late Majesty's Privy Council with numbers of other gentlemen of quality with the Lord Mayor of London and the aldermen and citizens of London.'

In 1952, the task of summoning the Accession Council fell to Sir Neville Leigh, then Senior Clerk to the Privy Council. He remembers a frantic morning, with hundreds of people to summon via a single bakelite telephone and the local telegraph office.

Late that afternoon, the 'great and the good', most of them clad in frock coats and top hats, entered St James's Palace, past guards already wearing black armbands, and assembled in quiet huddles in the dimly lit Picture Gallery. There were 191 of them.

On the tables, Sir Neville and his colleagues had laid out the Proclamation documents for signature and waited for the meeting to begin.

Punctually at 5 o'clock, Lord Woolton, who was then the Lord President of the Council, called for silence and invited the Clerk to read out the Proclamation.

I don't remember the exact words of it, but I remember it started with 'Whereas, it has pleased Almighty God to call unto his mercy . . .' And it went on like that, ending with a resounding 'God Save the Queen!', which the people present repeated, as I remember it.

After that had been done, we invited the people who were there to form up into queues to sign the Proclamation, which they did, most of them, with extremely antiquated dip-pens which fortunately managed to produce signatures which were legible enough for us to decipher afterwards.

The meeting then adjourned. Usually, after the signing of the Proclamation, the new monarch enters to make a formal declaration, but the Queen was 4,000 miles away in Kenya where she and the Duke of Edinburgh had been on tour. After the Queen's return two days later, the Council met again. Walter Bottomley MP, newly elected to the Privy Council, was among the crowd in the Throne Room.

The Queen returns to Heathrow Airport, London, from Kenya, after learning of the death of her father. A delegation of politicians, including Sir Anthony Eden, Clement Attlee and Prime Minister Winston Churchill, was on the tarmac to meet her.

From the balcony of Friary Court at St James's Palace, Garter King of Arms, Sir George Bellew, reads the proclamation announcing the Queen's accession to the throne. The Earl Marshal, the Duke of Norfolk, is on his left. Ahead of them lies the task of organizing the Coronation.

The door opened in this room and in she came, dressed in black, looking very well but, nevertheless, appreciating that it was a most sombre occasion. She clearly showed that she was distressed. She made a simple but clear speech and said that she would serve her country faithfully and well, which she has done ever since. And then at the end of that she took her departure and we all stood up and sent her off, happy in the knowledge that we were going to have a great Queen to rule over us for many years to come.

The Accession Council over, the scene was set for another ceremony, held later that grey and snowy morning at St James's Palace. Sombre though the occasion was, the reading of the Proclamation from the balcony of Friary Court was enlivened by the resplendent uniforms of the State

Trumpeters and the bright medieval colours of the heralds and pursuivants arrayed in their tabards of damask, satin and velvet, the symbols of their royal authority. The Duke of Norfolk, the Earl Marshal, was there too, but the centre of attention was Sir George Bellew, Garter King of Arms. At eleven o'clock, standing on a soapbox concealed behind the parapet, he unrolled the Proclamation and began to read. He recalls:

It was tremendously windy and I had this enormous document, the size of *The Times* newspaper, and the wind caught hold of it and of course it made it flap up. Fortunately, a King of Arms beside me had the presence of mind to catch hold of the corner and pull it down. But I was able to read unimpeded until I got three-quarters of the way through, when I realized I had got on to the wrong rails and I was reading the same line twice. However, I had the presence of mind to continue without any hesitation to read the same line twice, right to the end. After that, I was more careful to use my thumbs to guide me, but I don't think anybody noticed it.

An onlooker later described the scene:

Garter looked up from the parchment, raised his plumed hat high and cried, 'God Save the Queen'.

The trumpets began to sound with peal rising upon peal until their fanfares were merged in the rising notes of the National Anthem from the Coldstream Guards' band. When the last note faded away everyone stood in silence as though reluctant to leave the moment behind. Then the glittering pageantry on the balcony began to filter away through the open window. In the silence we could hear the distant crash of the guns firing the salute in Hyde Park.

So ended what should have been the first of many proclamations throughout Britain and the Commonwealth. But Canada had jumped the

By tradition, before the proclamation can be read in the City of London, the procession of heralds and soldiers must ask the Lord Mayor of London for permission to enter the Square Mile. Until this is granted, a silk cord bars their way.

The date of the Coronation is proclaimed on the steps of the Royal Exchange in London on 7 June 1952. Proclamations were once a well-used tool of monarchy. In today's world of mass-communications, only accessions, coronations and General Elections are announced in this way.

gun by announcing two days earlier, before the second meeting of the Accession Council, that 'our only lawful and rightful liege Lady' was now 'Elizabeth II by the grace of God, of Great Britain, Ireland and the British Dominions beyond the seas, Queen, Defender of the Faith, supreme Liege Lady in and over Canada.' In London, a procession moved off from St James's Palace for three more readings of the proclamation.

At Temple Bar it halted for another ceremony, dating back to the times of Queen Elizabeth I. A silk cord, strung across the entrance to the City, barred the way.

'Who comes there?' asked the City Marshal.

As tradition demanded, the answer came from one of the heralds, Portcullis Pursuivant:

'His Majesty's Officers of Arms who demand entrance into the City of London in order to proclaim her Royal Majesty Queen Elizabeth II.'

Only then was the herald admitted to the Lord Mayor's presence, and, once the Order in Council requiring the proclamation to be made had been handed over, Norroy and Ulster King of Arms stepped forward to announce the news to the waiting crowd.

Similar scenes, with local variations, were enacted throughout the country. In York, the Lord Mayor drank the new Queen's health from a gold cup, while in Edinburgh the Albany Herald notched up a unique record when he declaimed the proclamation by the water at Leith: he had performed this task for the four preceding monarchs, Edward VII, George V, Edward VIII and George VI.

Even in 1952, Royal Proclamations had long outlived their practical purpose of communicating a monarch's commands to his or her subjects. Newspapers and radio now carried out the job of heralds and town criers, more speedily if less quaintly. Once widely used to announce declarations of

In Edinburgh, Royal Proclamations are always read three or four days later than in London. The delay was caused by the time taken for a horseman to bring the document from England to the Scottish capital. Today, it is sent by post or fax. Here, the death of King George VI is proclaimed by Sir Thomas Innes of Learney. In February 1952 he was Scotland's senior herald, Lord Lyon King of Arms.

war and public celebrations, they had now become purely ceremonial, announcing only accessions, coronations and General Elections. Yet the ceremonies in February 1952 fulfilled a need. The King's death had come as a shock, and, for the people who heard them, the proclamations opened up a vista of brighter days in the new Elizabethan age.

Not all the ceremonies held later in 1952 were to inaugurate the new reign. In the City of London, the Trial of the Pyx was held as usual, as it has been, almost unchanged, in unbroken succession since 1248. The purpose of the Trial is to check that the Royal Mint is manufacturing the coinage of the realm to the right standard. Once held in the Inner Chamber next to the Star Chamber at Westminster, this medieval court is nowadays convened at the opulent Goldsmiths' Hall in the heart of London's financial district. The Trial begins with the ceremonial entry of the Queen's Remembrancer who swears in a jury made up of members of the Goldsmiths Company. In 1992, members included a former Chairman of Rolls Royce, a leading educationalist, experts on silver, a jeweller and a solicitor. Later, the Queen's Remembrancer, Master Topley, explained his part in the proceedings:

The Queen's Remembrancer takes part because he is the last vestigial remains of the old Court of the Exchequer. The record we have from the thirteenth century indicates that the coinage was tried by a jury in the presence of the Barons of the Exchequer who were the judges of the Court of the Exchequer. The Court of Exchequer, although abolished in the middle of the last century, has been left in being in two offices, that of the Queen's Remembrancer and the Chancellor of the Exchequer. And it is in that capacity that the trial is conducted before me. It wouldn't be appropriate to try it in the presence of the Chancellor of the Exchequer because he is Master of the Mint and, in a sense, he is the man in the dock.

The jury of more than 20 men and women sit at a long table. Before them are two bowls: one made of copper, the other of wood. Officials of

ABOVE: *At the Trial of the Pyx, coins chosen at random at the Royal Mint's factory in Wales must be unpacked and counted.*

the Royal Mint bring them packets of coins selected at random from the factory's total output of more than £84 million worth of currency. The packets are taken to London from Wales in wooden boxes – the Pyx.

First, the jurors have to count the coins in each packet. Then they choose one coin for laboratory testing. This they place in a copper bowl; the others go into the wooden one before being returned to the Pyx. The trial is, literally, a dazzling sight with silver, copper and gold flashing in the brightly lit livery hall against the backdrop of the magnificent treasures of the Goldsmiths Company.

The year 1992 was Master Topley's second as Queen's Remembrancer. He found the trial and its archaic trappings easy to justify:

It is necessary to have the framework of a trial because it is indeed a trial. It isn't simply the testing of the fineness of the coinage in the laboratory that needs to be gone into. The number of coins set aside must be tested and that is a counting enterprise, hence perhaps the rather large number of jurors that we have because there are so many coins to be counted. If the correct number of coins is not set aside in the Pyx, then we might have to start all over again. So we have this large number of jurors for that purpose. The weighing is done by the jurors, and the weighing in bulk is done by the jurors or by others under their immediate command. It is indeed in every way a trial, although the person in the dock is not a human being but the coinage of the realm.

Today, as in the past, the trial is taken seriously by the Royal Mint. When the coinage has proved defective, Masters have been known to be dismissed. In 1990 John Major, then Chancellor of the Exchequer, breathed a sigh of relief when the jury pronounced in his favour:

My officials have had great pleasure – malign pleasure, even malicious pleasure – in warning me of the dreadful fate that can befall Masters of the Mint when the coinage is found to be below standard. I gather that one Master in 1318 was sacked and jailed for six weeks for making a silver coin below standard, and another, 30 years later, was fined £93. 13s. 3d. I understand the penalties have been rather less in recent years, but I am nevertheless relieved that I have not had cause to find out what they are!

BELOW: *The task of the jury is to make a further choice and select the coins which will go for testing in the laboratories of the Goldsmiths Company.*

In 1992, Norman Lamont, John Major's successor as Chancellor, was not the only government official anxiously awaiting the verdict. George Gair, the High Commissioner of New Zealand, was on hand to watch the opening of the trial, because the coinage of his country is also produced by the Royal Mint. As he watched the jury bending to its blend of ancient ceremony and modern consumer science, that for more than seven centuries has ensured the survival of the trial of the Pyx, he commented:

I think perhaps that only the British have this flair for bringing history into a dimension and a form in modern times which is relevant, yet nevertheless lacks nothing in terms of its ability to compete in standards with the rest of the world.

And with that he left the scientists and assayers of the Goldsmiths Company to perform the tests in their laboratories and furnaces which would help the jury reach a favourable verdict three months later in the ceremonial year.

March

March is always a quiet month for ceremonial and in 1952 it offered welcome respite for the young woman who had suddenly found herself Queen. The days after the King's death in February had been busy. The start of the Queen's reign had been marked with meetings with delegations of politicians and Commonwealth representatives. The Kings of Sweden, Denmark and Greece had called to see her after the funeral. So had the Queen of the Netherlands, the West German Chancellor and the President of France. Ambassadors from all over the world made their way to Buckingham Palace with messages of condolence. The Prime Minister, Winston Churchill, had had the first of his regular weekly audiences at Clarence House, where the Queen and the Duke of Edinburgh were still living.

The Court was plunged into mourning: the women of the Royal Family and their Households wore black dresses. The men donned black ties with their most sombre suits. Letters were written on black-edged paper and all social invitations were refused. Yet, within the walls of the Queen's palaces and houses, the daily round of unobtrusive ceremonial continued unabated.

All the flags in London flew at half-mast when the Queen arrived home, except one. As she drove into Clarence House, the Royal Standard was run to the top of its mast. It signified that the Crown passes, without interruption, from one heartbeat to the next. The responsibility for this lay then, as now, with the Royal Flagman. He has to choose which flag to fly and the preparing and flying of the Royal Standard is a virtually full-time job. Lance-Sergeant Chalky White, who held the post in 1992, explains:

There are five different sizes of standard. The first one that we have is the six foot by three foot, which is mainly used for trips or visits that the Queen goes on. Then

The Royal Standard flies where the Queen goes. It is divided into four quarters. The three lions passant of England appear in two of them; the harp represents Ireland and the lion rampant Scotland. Wales is not included because it is a principality.

The Royal Standard over Buckingham Palace. In fact, there are several flags of different sizes. One is flown on great State occasions, another is for bad weather, yet another is designed for use at night.

we've got the nine foot by four-and-a-half Royal Standard. Then there's the twelve foot by six foot, which is the one that is normally flown at Buckingham Palace and Windsor Castle and various other Royal Households. The next size Standard up from that is an eighteen by nine which is flown at Royal Garden Parties here at Buckingham Palace and at the Palace of Holyroodhouse. The next one from that is the 24 by 12 which is flown on State Visits, and then there's the largest one, which is 36 foot by 18 and is flown at Trooping the Colour and Royal Weddings.

Whenever the Queen arrives at any of her palaces, the Flagman must be on the roof ready to break out the Royal Standard as soon as her car crosses the threshold. He takes pride in carrying out the ceremony with precise timing.

This is one of the more obvious examples of how British kings and queens have always communicated with their subjects through ceremony. The Royal Standard is a signal not only of the Queen's presence but also of where power and authority lie.

The job of preparing the Royal Standard is an elaborate affair. At Buckingham Palace, Sergeant White often has to leave it to dry in his room for several hours while the Night Standard is flying. Then he must find a room large enough in which to fold it: this, at least, presents no problems. He next concertinas it into a bundle before making his way via staircases and ladders to the roof of the Palace itself.

The view is breathtaking. London lies at his feet: the Mall stretching all the way to Admiralty Arch; the grassy acres of Green Park and St James's Park; the imposing government buildings in Whitehall, with the River Thames beyond. From here, Sergeant White, sheltering if need be from the weather in one of two wooden watchtowers and briefed about the likely time of her return, can invariably spot the Queen's car. The ritual never changes:

I go up to the flagpole, which is right on top of the roof. I attach the Royal Standard to the flagpole. I then move to a position where I can see which way the Queen is going to approach from. On seeing the Queen's car coming in through either the North centre gate or the South centre gate, I then go to pull the Royal Standard so it then flies in the wind.

With an immaculate salute from the rooftop beside his now proudly streaming Royal Standard, Lance-Sergeant White returns to earth and to his other duties about the Palace.

In March 1952, one ancient ceremony could not be delayed, for this is the month in which the Lists of the High Sheriffs of England are always pricked. The ceremony takes place at a meeting of the Privy Council. The names of the candidates for these prestigious, but now almost entirely symbolic posts, are inscribed on a long roll which is presented to the Queen by the Clerk of the Privy Council. He then hands her a 'bodkin' – a spike with a handle on it – which she uses to prick a hole against the names of the people who will be next year's High Sheriffs. Three names are offered for each post, but the top one is invariably chosen, with the other two taking 'Buggins' turn' in the two succeeding years.

No one knows exactly how the tradition of pricking arose. According to legend, Queen Elizabeth I was presented with the list while she was sewing. Since she had no pen to hand, she used a needle to make her mark, where-as her predecessors had always settled for a black ink dot.

Whatever its origins, list-pricking became the conventional way of choosing High Sheriffs. At a separate private audience with the Chancellor of the Duchy of Lancaster, the Queen does the same for her own lands in

The Royal Standard must be carefully concertinaed into a bundle before being taken to the roof. Fortunately, Lance-Sergeant White has a large choice of rooms at Buckingham Palace for this part of the ritual.

the North of England. However, there are signs that the days of these eccentric ceremonies may be numbered, for the Prince of Wales no longer pricks the list of his Duchy of Cornwall.

In 1992, the pricking of the lists of the Duchy of Lancaster was a hastily arranged affair, for its Chancellor, Chris Patten, had other pressing concerns. Prime Minister John Major had called a General Election and Chris Patten knew that, as Chairman of the Conservative Party and the holder of a marginal seat in Parliament, he would have little time for anything beyond campaigning. But for others, the General Election sparked off a series of ceremonies outside their normal routine.

The two chief players were Geoffrey de Deney, the Clerk of the Privy Council, and Tom Legg, the Clerk to the Crown in Chancery. For Legg it was his first General Election after becoming Chief Executive of the Lord Chancellor's Department, responsible for the administration of the judiciary, a staff of 12,000 and a budget of more than £1 billion a year. For de Deney, the Election in 1992 was his last before retirement. Legg summed up the task ahead:

The calling of the Election has had three consequences for us. First of all, we had to issue the writs which caused the elections for the House of Commons to happen. They first have to be written with the names of the constituencies inserted onto the writ. Then they have to be sealed and they have to be put into envelopes, together with accompanying material, and handed over to the Post Office for delivery. This sounds simple, and in principle it is simple, but you will appreciate that we have to get it absolutely right. There must be no mistakes about this at all.

Then we have to prepare the writs for the peers of the House of Lords: that's to say, the writs of Summons to peers, bishops and judges, all of whom receive summonses to the House of Lords, and they, too, have to be handed over to the Post Office for delivery.

RIGHT: *John Bartrip, the Sealer of the Realm in 1992. The Great Seal always used to be moulded in a silver matrix. Today, for speed and convenience, this laborious process has been replaced in many cases by the use of the 'wafer' Seal, which only has to be impressed onto the paper.*

BELOW: *The very moment at which Parliament was dissolved before the 1992 General Election. The impress of the Great Seal of the Realm on the Dissolution Proclamation makes the whole thing official.*

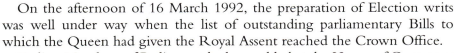

The second thing we have to do is to arrange for the great Seal to be affixed to the Commission for the Prorogation of Parliament and the giving of the Royal Assent to those Bills which are ready. We also have to put the Great Seal onto the Proclamation which dissolves Parliament and brings it to an end, so that the Election can happen.

Finally, we have to begin to get ready to receive the writs back again after the Election has taken place.

On the afternoon of 16 March 1992, the preparation of Election writs was well under way when the list of outstanding parliamentary Bills to which the Queen had given the Royal Assent reached the Crown Office.

Earlier, Members of Parliament had assembled at the House of Commons for the last day of business. Among them was the Member for Finchley, the former Prime Minister, Mrs Margaret Thatcher. For her and many of her colleagues it was a sad day, for they had decided to retire, leaving their seats to be contested by younger political hopefuls.

There was just time for Tom Legg to check with his assistant Jenny Waine that the Bills had, in fact, completed their passage through Parliament. Then he was off to the Chamber of the House of Lords:

My own role in the Prorogation Ceremony is to take part in that section of it which authenticates the giving of the Royal Assent to Acts of Parliament. I do this together with the Clerk of the Parliaments. When the Queen's Commission to prorogue Parliament and give the Royal Assent has been read out to the House of Lords, with the House of Commons also present, I then stand up with a list of the Bills which are ready for the Royal Assent. I read out the name of each Bill, and, as I read out its name, so at that moment the Clerk of the Parliaments turns around and speaks to the House of Commons who are standing at the Bar of the House of Lords and says the Norman French formula which indicates that the Queen has assented to that Bill.

Despite its great weight, the matrix of the Great Seal was always carried in an elaborately woven purse by the Lord Chancellor. This had unfortunate repercussions. In the eighteenth century, one Lord Chancellor dropped it onto his foot and broke a bone. In Queen Victoria's reign, the custom of presenting a new purse to the Lord Chancellor every year was discontinued: there were so many old ones that the wife of at least one Lord Chancellor caused scandal by recycling hers into curtains.

BELOW: *Mr Speaker, Bernard Weatherill, prorogues Parliament before the 1992 General Election. This marks the end of business at Westminster, but Parliament was not actually dissolved until the Dissolution Proclamation was sealed later that evening.*

The ceremony has survived, Legg says, because Parliament enjoys it:

The old-fashioned Ceremony of Prorogation is no longer necessary as a matter of law. It is not required because, ever since 1967, it has been possible for the Royal Assent to be signified by a more informal procedure, by which the Speaker and the Lord Chancellor simply announce to their respective houses that the Royal Assent has been given. But at the time when that new procedure was introduced, Parliament made it clear that it did want the old procedure to be continued from time to time. So it does happen at least once a year and, typically, when a General Election is called.

When the last '*La Reine le veult*' had been pronounced, the Lords dispersed into the afternoon darkness and the Commons returned to its own chamber for one last ritual.

One by one, they shook the hand of the Speaker, Bernard Wetherill, who was retiring. Then those who hoped to return headed for the hustings, while the old-stagers began to dream of the price their memoirs might fetch. The Chambers lay empty, but Parliament still had not been dissolved. This can only be done when the Dissolution Proclamation has been approved by the Privy Council, signed by the Queen, and sealed.

Nothing can become law without being affixed with the Great Seal of the Realm. The Seal has been used to authenticate documents since at least the eleventh century when monarchs realized that its use might prevent forgery and political chicanery.

Today, the Seal can be applied in two ways. The first, traditional method, is to take two moulded silver plates, the matrix, and fill them with wax or plastic granules. A cord for attaching to the document to be sealed sticks out of the mould. Since this can be a lengthy process – it can take some hours for the Seal to cool – a modern single-sided 'wafer' Seal usually takes its place. It can be impressed directly onto the paper.

Over the centuries, kings and queens and their keepers of the Great Seal, the Lord Chancellors, have guarded the matrix jealously. Edward III made counterfeiting it an act of high treason, while James II threw his Great Seal into the River Thames when he fled England in 1688, in the fruitless hope of thereby making the country ungovernable.

It is the replacing of the Great Seal that is one of the first things to which a new monarch always gives thought. There is a new one for each reign. Thus, in March 1952, the Duke of Edinburgh was appointed president of a committee charged with creating a new design. The Great Seal of King George VI continued to be used in the meantime, but, when its replacement finally appeared in August 1953, the old one was defaced, or 'damasked', by the Queen with a special hammer. Traditionally, half the defunct matrix is presented to the serving Lord Chancellor.

One side of the Great Seal of Elizabeth II shows the Queen robed and sitting on her throne. The other, which is also used in the wafer seal, depicts her on horseback, wearing the uniform of Colonel-in-Chief of the Grenadier Guards

Without the Great Seal of the Realm, laws cannot be made. Monarchs therefore guard it jealously. George III's was stolen by politicians trying to prevent him from dissolving Parliament. But the king outwitted them by having a new one made. Charles I's Great Seal was recognized as the key to the government of the country and was consequently bitterly fought over by Royalists and Parliamentarians in the English Civil War.

It was 6.18 p.m. before Geoffrey de Deney reached the House of Lords with the Dissolution Proclamation. Up in the lift he went and down the deserted corridors until he came to the unprepossessing white-painted room in which Parliament is dissolved. For waiting for him was John Bartrip, the man who affixes the Great Seal of the Realm. Slowly and precisely, John placed the Proclamation beneath the press. Then, after one final check, he levered the seal onto the paper. Hours after MPs thought Parliament had been dissolved, the deed was in fact done. It was 6.27 p.m. But one last pre-Election ritual still had to be enacted.

Three days later, the Proclamation had to be read to the people of Scotland from the Mercat Cross in Edinburgh. The clouds were dark and low, but the procession to the Mercat Cross brought colour enough to the dour High Street. The pipes and drums of a military band never fail to stir the soul, and the soldiers' appearance drew crowds as the ceremony approached.

Outside the Sheriff Court House stood the imposing figure of Sir Malcolm Innes of Edingight, Lord Lyon King of Arms and Scotland's premier herald. At precisely 11.45 a.m., the band and Guard of Honour halted opposite the Court House door, from which the Lyon Court Trumpeters at once emerged. Then, after the first six bars of the National Anthem, the procession moved off again. Past the dark mass of St Giles Cathedral it went, at a slow march. High above, the minute hand of the great clock moved inexorably towards noon. The Lord Lyon, arrayed in his bright tabard and flanked by the Officers of Arms and the Macer, marched between the ranks of the Guard of Honour.

The Mercat Cross was just a few yards away. Once there, the band wheeled right to face the City Chambers. As the Lord Lyon's procession continued into the base of the Mercat Cross, the Guard of Honour turned and shouldered arms. Almost immediately, the Lord Lyon and his retinue reappeared up on the platform.

There was silence. At last, when the clock had chimed the last notes of noon and the trumpeters had sounded a fanfare, Sir Malcolm began to deliver the news of the forthcoming election to the people of Scotland.

The Egyptian sun god Horus depicted in a papyrus from 1250 BC. Masks of his hawk-like head were worn by the messengers of the Pharaohs to give their pronouncements royal authority.

Afterwards, Sir Malcolm explained why the proclamation is read later in Scotland than in England:

In the past it took nearly three days for a galloper to come with a proclamation from London, and that is why it's often made roughly three or four days later in Edinburgh.

The Lord Lyon's 'playing card' tabard gives him the authority of the Crown:

One wears the tabard to make the proclamation because, by putting on the Royal Arms, which almost indicate that one is part of the royal presence, one's individual persona disappears and one takes on the persona of the Sovereign. So, in one sense, one speaks with the Sovereign's voice. The origin of this can be traced back into the far period of history of the time of the Pharaohs on the Upper Nile, when the mask of Horus was placed over the person's head and he then spoke with the voice of the incarnate Sovereign.

These days, the text arrives by post or fax, and in an age of mass-media only the love of ceremony ensures the perpetuation of an enjoyable tradition:

The proclamation does not really require to be heard by people for legal effect. But we make it, I think, because people are in the middle of this frenetic time of an election, with rival manifestos and all the razzamatazz, and I think they like to pause for a moment and reflect on the constitutional position and be reminded, perhaps, of the struggle to get the vote and how really serious is their action in the election later on.

Life would undoubtedly be less colourful, and my impression is that the people of Scotland like to see the modest, authentic ceremonial done with dignity, and I understand it gives them great satisfaction to see it done.

As Lord Lyon's procession returned to the Court House, a heckler from the crowd shouted, 'What do we want with all this stuff from England's Parliament?' The politics had begun!

April

The month of April in 1952 and 1992 was one of decisions.

Since the King's death in February 1952, the Cabinet had been trying to agree upon a date for the Coronation. The newspapers, impatient to tap what they saw as an endless spring of good copy, were clamouring for it to be held at the earliest possible opportunity. As a result, some fanatical royal-watchers, anxious not to miss a moment's pomp and pageantry, optimistically booked hotel rooms for 'dead cert' dates in the summer.

However, the Minister of Works, David Eccles, would not be rushed. Straight after the King's funeral, he had sent for the files of the previous coronation, held in 1937. They were voluminous and crammed with detail. There were route maps, carpet samples, the names and addresses of people entitled to tickets, designs for decorations and temporary buildings, maps of sewage systems for tented army camps, orders for fieldsful of flowers . . . The days when a new monarch had to be crowned speedily to secure the throne were long gone. Besides, Eccles argued, the chance to attract tourists from all over the world to a country still impoverished by a world war should not be cast aside.

A viewing of the film of the 1937 coronation confirmed the Minister's view: the supreme royal ceremony demanded careful preparation. Queen Victoria's coronation had taken 13 months to plan. Queen Elizabeth's, in a more complex world, would take at least as long. The Cabinet agreed. The diary kept by Eccles' ministry records:

On 8 April, 1952, the Cabinet discussed the exact date of the Coronation and decided to recommend a date between 29 May and 6 June 1953. The Cabinet were notified on 16 April 1952, that Her Majesty's Coronation would take place on 2 June 1953.

Eccles was determined to do things his way. The stuffy bureaucracy that had complicated the organization of previous coronations was not for him.

All that's laid down in law. You start off with a grand committee – a Royal Duke in the chair, the Archbishop of Canterbury, the Home Secretary and all the other bigwigs. And I was told that I had to wear a morning suit at each meeting. Well, I didn't like that, but I did it.

Of course, the real work, that's done just by two people. The Earl Marshal, that is the Duke of Norfolk of the time, has overall responsibility for the preparations by hereditary right. But he has to have a handyman, and it also had been laid down for generations and generations that he has to be the Minister of Works. It's the oldest office in the British government, dating back to 1100.

I was that Minister of Works, and, of course, everybody said, 'Well, you're going to quarrel a great deal with the Duke of Norfolk.' But we didn't. We didn't quarrel at all and I admired very much his capacity to deal with all those nosy-parkers and would-be helpers who came along.

Eccles revelled in the problems he encountered almost every hour of the day at the Ministry and, more often than not, dealt with them personally:

BELOW: *The Earl Marshal's 'handyman'. David Eccles, Minister of Works at the time of the Coronation, used elaborate charts to keep track of the countless tasks involved in the organization of the great spectacle.*

At a press conference at Church House, Westminster, David Eccles explains his plans. The map of the processional route was redrawn to enable as many people as possible to watch the pageantry.

They said I ought to have an advisory committee of distinguished architects and artists. Well, I refused point-blank, because I knew they'd argue from morning to night, and we'd never be ready on time. So I had to take a risk and rely on my own judgement and that of my excellent staff.

We had great progress charts all over the wall showing each contract and when it had to be fulfilled, because you must remember we were working against the clock. I was told, 'Look out, because the last fortnight you'll find the workmen will strike.' Of course they didn't strike, but they told me they would. It was really very remarkable; I was at one time dealing with a hundred or more contracts every morning.

Nothing could be overlooked and the most basic problems had to be meticulously researched. Thus it was that a man from the Ministry found himself visiting a consultant urologist in Harley Street one morning. His mission: to discover how often men and women need to use the lavatory in seven hours. This was the length of time the ticket-holders would have to spend incarcerated in Westminster Abbey on Coronation day. Armed with expert opinion, the unblushing official was able to make an informed guess as to the number of lavatories that would be needed.

The Earl Marshal, too, was already hard at work. The first thing he needed was an office. He had organized the funeral of George V from Norfolk House, the coronation of George VI from rooms in Buckingham Palace Road and February's obsequies from St James's Palace. But none of these was available. Naturally he turned to his 'handyman', and an imposing house in Mayfair was found and requisitioned for him by the Ministry of Works.

By now, Garter King of Arms, Sir George Bellew, was on the Duke's staff. He remembered his first visit to 14 Belgrave Square:

When I went with the Earl Marshal to inspect it and to allocate rooms to his various administrative officers and heads of departments, I was struck by his apparent knowledge of its lay-out.

'You seem to know the geography of this house.' I observed conversationally.

'Yes,' he replied, 'it belongs to me, actually. I spent some of my early youth here.'

In April 1992, the decisions were made by the voters of the United Kingdom at a General Election. Voting was held on 9 April, and, after a three-week lull – if such a term can be used in connection with the hurly-burly of the hustings – the train of ceremonies, which had begun with the Dissolution of Parliament in March, approached its end.

In the small hours of the morning, in town halls, leisure centres, schools and public rooms all over the kingdom, the results in each constituency were read out by the Returning Officers. These men and women, usually Sheriffs, Mayors or Deputy Sheriffs, are representatives of the Crown. For a few brief moments, Returning Officers like Geoffrey Key in Sunderland, the winner of the race to declare the first result in 1992, can bask in the national limelight as they reveal the fate of the exhausted candidates behind them. Their script is formal, their bearing dignified, their robes of office or the sombre cut of their suits lending authority to their pronouncements. Yet the declaration itself is less important ceremonially than their final duty. This is usually carried out once the cheers for the victor and the stiff-upper-lipped platitudes of the losers' speeches have died away. As the hall empties, the Returning Officer writes the name of the newly elected Member of Parliament on the back of the writ: it is this that will give him or her the right to a seat in the House of Commons.

At the Crown Office in the House of Lords, the committee room used to draw up the writs before the Election was once again pressed into service. There, the Clerk of the Chamber, Jenny Waine, and her helpers spent the weekend compiling two 'white books'. One, listing all 651 constituencies of the United Kingdom and the names and addresses of each MP, was for Crown Office records. The other, without the addresses, would be used in 18 days' time at the Summoning of Parliament.

The Summoning is one of the most laborious of all ceremonies and can last up to three days. On 27 April, the Royal Commissioners, sitting on a bench in front of the Woolsack, opened the proceedings by commanding the Commons to appear before the Lord Chancellor in the House of Lords. By convention, only one MP ever turns up. He is always the longest serving member or 'Father of the House': in 1992 the honour fell to the former Prime Minister, Sir Edward Heath. Then the Lord Chancellor rose to repeat the ancient formula that sets out the first tasks of the new Parliament: the swearing in of all MPs and the election of a new Speaker.

My Lords and Members of the House of Commons, we have it in command from Her Majesty to let you know that, as soon as Members of both Houses shall be sworn, the causes of Her Majesty calling this Parliament will be declared to you: and it being necessary that a Speaker of the House of Commons should be first chosen, it is Her Majesty's pleasure that you, Members of the Commons, repair and proceed to the choice of some proper person to be your Speaker and that you present such person here, tomorrow, for Her Majesty's Royal Approbation.

A few days earlier, on Monday, 13 April, behind closed doors in Buckingham Palace, members of Prime Minister John Major's new Cabinet had gathered to receive their Seals of Office from the Queen at a meeting of the Privy Council. They looked excited as they met in the Bow Room: victory had been unexpected and consequently the sweeter. Many of them had spent the weekend in their constituencies sleeping off the campaign. This was the first chance to savour their triumph with their colleagues.

Geoffrey de Deney, the Clerk to the Privy Council, and his deputy, Robert Bulling, moved from huddle to huddle, handing out red–bound copies of the New Testament on which, in a few minutes' time, the new ministers would swear their oath of office as Privy Counsellors. De Deney and Bulling had spent the morning gathering in the Seals from outgoing ministers, answering queries from new recruits anxious to comply with the Palace dress code, and digging out a suitable Seal for David Mellor's newly created Ministry for the National Heritage.

The two men also had to instruct the newcomers in the finer points of the ritual about to unfold. 'Kissing hands' is by no means as simple as it sounds. Rules have been laid down. First the minister kneels on a stool to take the oath. Then the Queen holds out her right hand, palm downwards and with her fingers together. The minister must then kiss it 'gently', holding it lightly in his hand and briefly brushing it with his lips: anything more vigorous would be deemed inappropriate.

Suddenly an electric bell rang. The Queen was ready to meet her Privy Council in the adjoining 1844 Room. The double doors opened and the

Jesus washing the feet of St Peter as depicted by the Victorian painter Ford Madox Brown. Christ's act of humility and love is the inspiration behind the service of Royal Maundy.

new Cabinet filed in. On a table next to the Queen the red Seal boxes could be glimpsed. Then the doors closed and the first Privy Council of the new Parliament went into private session.

By passing the Seals of Office to the new ministers, the Queen performs the simplest ceremony of constitutional monarchy. All power in Britain is vested in the Sovereign. Nothing can be done without invoking her authority. However, as Britain is a modern parliamentary democracy, the Queen passes her power symbolically through these Seals to the men and women chosen from the political party which has won the greatest public support in the polls. It is a simple, dignified and symbolic delivery of power.

Within minutes, it was over. Ministers had 'kissed hands', new members of the Privy Council had been sworn in. Pausing only to greet functionaries from the Royal Household who had dropped by, the politicians made briskly for the Grand Entrance where their official cars were waiting to take them back to Whitehall and the heady business of exercising power.

On 16 April, Mercia Tapsell and Bert Sandbach had a rather more public meeting with the Queen. Mercia and Bert had been chosen to take part in Royal Maundy, one of the oldest and most solemn royal ceremonies still performed today. Held on the Thursday before Easter, it was the Queen's first public engagement after her accession in 1952 and, with only four exceptions, she has attended every service since.

No one knows when it first became the custom for British kings and queens to wash the feet of some of their subjects, but the origins of the ceremony can be found in the Bible, in St John's description of Jesus at the Last Supper:

He riseth from supper and laid aside his garments and took a towel and girded himself. After that he poureth water into a basin, and began to wash the disciples' feet, and to wipe them with the towel wherewith he was girded.

Jesus explained his actions thus:

Verily, verily I say unto you, The servant is not greater than his Lord, neither he that is sent greater than he that sent him. . .

A new commandment I give unto you, That ye love one another; as I have loved you, that ye also love one another.

It is from this that the ceremony gets its name: 'Maundy' is a corruption of *mandatum* which is the Latin for 'commandment'.

A form of Maundy service, in which monks washed the feet of the poor after the Communion service on the Thursday before Easter, can be traced back to the fifth century. St Augustine, writing in 600AD, mentions it too. By 1213, the ceremony had become a royal one, with King John taking part. Poor people were chosen to have their feet washed and gifts of food, money and clothing – usually from the monarch's own back – were added, although there were fears that the Sovereign might catch the plague from the unsavoury feet of the great unwashed.

In the sixteenth century, Queen Mary I went to extraordinary lengths to follow Christ's example. A recent history by Peter A. Wright, Secretary to the Royal Almonry, describes how she took,

A miniature of Queen Elizabeth I at Royal Maundy, attributed to Nicholas Hilliard. Rather than part with a gown, she gave money to the recipients.

. . . special trouble to find the most worthy recipient for her gown of the finest purple cloth, lined with martens' fur, with sleeves 'so long and wide they reached the ground'. After going the whole length of the hall 'from one end to the other ever on her knees' in the ceremony of washing the women's feet, the Queen went twice round the hall, examining very closely all the poor women one by one, and then returning for the third time 'she gave the said gown to the one who was in fact the poorest and most aged of them all'.

Elizabeth I, vain as ever, substituted cash for the clothing to avoid parting with one of her gowns, and, in 1724, squabbles among the female recipients, all keen to try on the same royal garment, led to the abandonment of this part of the distribution.

Later, from the eighteenth century onwards, royal interest in the Maundy service became spasmodic. But in 1932 George V revived the custom of the sovereign distributing the purses. The Queen has made a further important change: Royal Maundy, once always held in London, now regularly 'moves' to provincial cathedrals, such as Chester where the service was held in 1992.

Thus it was that an important-looking letter arrived at Bert Sandbach's bungalow in Northwich in 1992. It told him that he had been chosen as a Maundy recipient:

The postman knocked me up at seven o'clock one morning and I answered the door to him. And there he was with a letter for me. He didn't like to put it through the door and he couldn't bend it. It had BUCKINGHAM PALACE on the back of it, so that set me wondering.

When I opened it and found out what it was – oh – I was over the moon. My legs went from under me near enough, as I wondered what I had done and who had put me in that position.

It turned out that Bert had been chosen as a reward for his work with a church charity. Mercia Tapsell became a recipient because she was a stalwart of another worthy body, the Salvation Army. They are typical of people nominated as Maundy recipients in modern times: charity cases have been replaced by the charitable.

Mercia Tapsell, like Bert Sandbach, felt privileged to be chosen to take part in an ancient ceremony she believed still had deep significance in modern life:

I think it has a great deal of relevance today, just to have our monarch come among us. I believe it is a special ceremony for her and I think it will stir the hearts of people in Chester, just the very fact that she is coming among us to give us this money. I think it will make them think. Surely in this world today, with so many non-thinkers and people who don't think about Christ, they will think, 'Now why has she come? Why has she done it?'

And I think it will be a good thing for the people of Chester just to have their thoughts turned to the Maundy service and what it symbolises.

I feel absolutely overwhelmed, really. I have 'collected' royalty ever since I was a little girl and my scrapbook goes right back to Albert and Victoria and that's the closest I ever thought of getting to royalty. But when I had the invitation that I was actually going to meet the Queen and receive the Maundy money, it just seemed to be beyond my wildest dreams. I didn't think it could happen to people like me.

One group of people finds the night before Royal Maundy particularly hectic. For more than 30 years, Mrs Valerie Bennett-Levy has been making the nosegays carried during the service. Today, these bunches of sweet-smelling flowers are simply decorative but they used to have a more sinister purpose: to ward off plague.

They must be fresh, so Mrs Bennett-Levy and her helpers labour through the night to wire the fresh flowers and herbs together and surround them with a lace doily.

In Chester, in the appropriately named Blossoms Hotel, work on preparing the nosegays began at ten o'clock and continued into the small hours.

Two Yeomen of the Guard act as the Dish Carriers. The golden dishes come from the Crown Jewels kept at the Tower of London. The Royal Almonry place the red and white purses in pairs for ease of distribution by the Queen.

The 'recipe' never changes. Into each nosegay go:

9 daffodils	12 bunches of primroses
11 pieces of white stock	20 pieces of cupressus
15 cheerfulness	14 sprigs of rosemary
14 bunches of violets	12 sprigs of thyme

As a fine day dawned over Chester, everything was ready. Long before the service, the cathedral began to fill. The 132 recipients – one man and one woman for every year of the Queen's age – were checking where they had to sit. Singers from the Chapel Royal Choir mingled with local choristers. Officials from the Royal Almonry office at Buckingham Palace laid out the purses of money to be distributed on vast silver-gilt dishes carried in the procession by members of the Yeomen of the Guard. In the past, recipients were paid in kind with bread and fish instead of money. Because of the dreadful smell, the dishes of fish were carried on the Yeomen of the Guard's heads. Today these dishes are still carried in the same manner, with the purse strings hanging down like rats' tails, all around the edge.

In the Consistory Court near the West Door, the Lord High Almoner, the Bishop of St Albans, donned the towels once used in the washing of feet.

Just before the service, three processions entered. From the Lady Chapel came the Honorary Canons and Rural Deans. From the West Door, came the main procession, led by the Crucifer and Taperers of the cathedral. Behind them walked choristers, representatives of local churches, the Bishop of Chester and his Chaplain, the Cathedral Architect who looks after the building, the Queen, the Duke of Edinburgh and the Lord Lieutenant for Cheshire. The rafters rang with the opening hymn:

> All my hope on God is founded;
> He doth still my trust renew . . .

Then from the Consistory Court came the staff of the Royal Almonry, holders of offices both quaintly named and redolent of bygone days: the Clerk of the Cheque and Adjutant, the Wandsmen, who command the Yeoman of the Guard, the Serjeant of the Vestry of Her Majesty's Chapel Royal, the Sub Almoner and Lord High Almoner. With them, carrying nosegays, walked the four Children of the Royal Almonry. Today they come from local schools, but in the past, rather grotesquely, the 'Children' were old men who helped with the foot washing.

The descant echoed to a conclusion and, in the silence, the Lord High Almoner, like his predecessors of more than eight centuries before, spoke the words of the *mandatum* which lie at the heart of Royal Maundy: 'Jesus said "I give you a new commandment: Love one another; as I have loved you, so you are to love one another."'

The psalm took up the theme, 'For though the Lord be high, yet hath he respect unto the lowly.'

It was echoed in the prayers:

Lord Jesus Christ, who before instituting the Holy Sacrament at thy Last

A group photograph is a new tradition at Royal Maundy. The Children of the Royal Almonry share the limelight with the Queen and the Duke of Edinburgh and the clergy who officiated at the service.

Supper, washed the feet of thine Apostles; teach us, by thine example, the grace of humility . . .

And in the anthems: 'Wash me thoroughly from my wickedness, and forgive me all my sin . . .'

The Queen, flanked by the Lord High Almoner and the Yeomen of the Guard, then distributed the Maundy Money: first to recipients on the south side of the Cathedral, then to those on the north.

After the service, at lunch at the Grosvenor Hotel below the cathedral, Bert Sandbach was at last able to satisfy his curiosity and open the purses. The red one contained £5.50: £3 for clothing, £1.50 for food, and £1 to make up for his not getting a part of the Queen's gown.

The white purse held the Maundy Money: 66 pence, one for every year of the Queen's age. First minted in 1662 during the reign of Charles II, the coins are specially designed and produced, making them so sought-after by collectors and dealers that the names of the recipients are a closely guarded secret. It was not always so, however: in the nineteenth century anyone could buy a set through a bank.

Mercia Tapsell died suddenly in July 1992 at the age of 71, her last months illuminated by her memories of Royal Maundy and the emotions of the day:

It surpassed anything that I ever thought. I didn't ever think that I should be in the cathedral with the Queen and all the dignitaries that were there. And the singing, the organ, the Queen, just everything and everybody. It's really been out of this world. Just to hear *Zadok the Priest*, I think, has lifted me to Cloud Nine, because it's something that I love. And to hear that and to have the Queen pass so close to me. And yes, she smiled. She smiled at me.

THE CEREMONIES
OF SUMMER

Somebody said that Britain may have lost out on a number of things, but we can still show the world a clean pair of heels when it comes to ceremonial.

The *Daily Mirror* on the Queen's Silver Jubilee 8 June 1977

May

CORONATIONS seldom run smoothly. This is one of the lessons of history.

When he was crowned on Christmas Day 1066, William the Conqueror insisted that the Abbey congregation should proclaim him king in both English and French. But the bilingual shouts panicked the guards outside, who, fearful that a rebellion was underway, decided to restore security by setting fire to all the neighbouring houses. In September 1189 a massacre of

The coronation of George IV was the most spectacular ever held, but it was not without its problems. The organizers had to disguise prize fighters as pages to quell the unruly behaviour of guests in the Abbey.

Jewish leaders from the City of London blighted Richard I's coronation, while Henry III had to be 'crowned' with one of his mother's bracelets in the unavoidable absence of the proper article which King John had lost in the Wash.

Ten-year-old Richard II was so tired out by the proceedings that he had to be carried home to his palace, losing a shoe somewhere on the way. When Anne Boleyn became queen in 1533 her pregnancy made her incontinent and she had to be attended by ladies with chamber-pots, while Charles I stumbled on his arrival at the Abbey – a bad omen for an ill-fated reign.

At Charles II's coronation in 1651, the congregation was bored into near stupefaction by the reading of a comprehensive list of every King and Queen of England there had ever been. James II's was chaotic. In one of the processions, the new monarch's crown almost fell off. The King's Champion slipped and fell as he dismounted to kiss his Sovereign's hand and then lay helpless on the ground, weighed down by his elaborate suit of armour.

Even that most magnificent of all coronations, George IV's in 1821, was marred by the rowdiness of the guests who had to be kept under control by prizefighters disguised as pages.

Queen Victoria was crowned in 1838 amid a series of farcical mishaps. The writer Harriet Martineau described how Lord Rolle collapsed while paying homage:

The large, infirm old man was held up by two peers, and had nearly reached the royal footstool when he slipped through the hands of his supporters, and rolled over and over down the steps, lying at the bottom coiled up in his robes.

Rather tartly, Martineau observed:

A foreigner in London gravely reported to his own countrymen, what he entirely believed on the word of a wag, that the Lords Rolle held their title on the condition of performing the feat at every Coronation . . .

The new Queen was barely more restrained in her journal. She was scandalized by the state of the St Edward's Chapel and the Archbishop of Canterbury's lackadaisical approach to the service:

What was *called* an *Altar* was covered with sandwiches, bottles of wine etc. The Archbishop came in and *ought* to have delivered the Orb to me, but I had already got it. There we waited for some minutes; Lord Melbourne took a glass of wine, for he seemed completely tired; the Procession being formed, I replaced my Crown (which I had taken off for a few minutes), took the Orb in my left hand and the Sceptre in my right, and thus *loaded* proceeded through the Abbey, which resounded with cheers, to the first Robing-room.

Later, the Archbishop forced the ring onto the wrong finger. It proved painful, indeed almost impossible, to take off.

Events went only marginally more smoothly in the twentieth century. In 1902, not only did the Archbishop of Canterbury stumble and have to be caught by nearby bishops, but he almost placed the crown on Edward VII's head the wrong way round. Queen Alexandra suffered the indignity of being anointed with so much oil that it soused her hair and ran down her nose. King George VI, in 1937, had to buckle the belt of the Sword of State himself because the hands of the Lord Chamberlain, who traditionally does the job, were shaking so violently, and for several heart-stopping moments the Archbishop of Canterbury fumbled anxiously with the crown as he checked that he had got it the right way round.

In 1952, with the Coronation barely a year away, the organizers, with the vociferous exception of David Eccles, clearly believed that the way to prevent disaster was to form committees. In fact, there were so many that it proved difficult to find names to distinguish them. Nevertheless, the Coronation Committee of the Privy Council, the Coronation Executive Committee, the Coronation Joint Committee, the Ministry of Works Coronation Committee, the Earl Marshal's Liaison Committee, the Dean of Westminster's Committee, and, in their turn, the multifarious sub-committees that they spawned, all diligently considered every aspect of the great spectacular.

First off the mark was the Cabinet Committee on Coronation Preparations. This began work as soon as the King's funeral was over. Although it dealt with 'a variety of matters which were of special interest to Ministers' such as television and the dress regulations for the Abbey service, its main task was to draw up a budget.

Using figures based on the costs of the coronation in 1937, the Committee's first estimate was £863,000. But by May 1952, it was already

clear that this was too low, and the final budget, approved later in the year, amounted to a more realistic £1,292,150.

In fact, the final bill, totted up long after the tumult and the shouting, proved to be very much lower. Prudent spending ensured that the Coronation came in £30,000 under budget and the huge sum of £684,050 was recouped by selling off everything that could be sold. Many a church later boasted its own stretch of Abbey carpet, acquired at £4 per square yard, and the stately homes of England, Scotland and Wales were filled with Abbey chairs. The doors of the Annexe were sold to Garter King of Arms for £100 and every last plank was disposed of to builders.

Almost half the budget was earmarked for building and decorating stands along the processional route and a further £297,100 for preparing Westminster Abbey. The largest sums – the £695,000 for the stands, £126,300 for decorating and floodlighting the streets of London and £51,000 for the construction of the Annexe, a temporary building at the entrance to the Abbey – were allocated to one man. Eric Bedford, the Ministry of Works' Chief Architect, had had more notice than most of the task ahead. On the morning of the King's death, at a meeting called to discuss the funeral arrangements, talk had turned to the Coronation of the new Queen. By May 1952, Bedford and his team were hard at work. Hard was the operative word: in the whole year before the Coronation, the Chief Architect was able to take only two days off.

Bedford watched the Ministry of Works screening of the 1937 Coronation film with intense interest and immediately decided to make changes. The first was to decorate The Mall, the grandiose approach to Buckingham Palace, in a style more suited to the pomp, pageantry and glitter of the occasion. The 1937 effort – conventional flag poles linked with strings of garish bunting – he dismissed as 'hanging out the washing'.

Bedford was heir to a long and magnificent tradition. For many centuries, the citizens of London have ensured that their city has provided a setting worthy of the most dazzling of royal ceremonies. The scenes still leap undimmed from the pages of the history books.

On the day before his coronation, Richard II rode out from the Tower on the finest charger to be found in all the acres of his new realm. Dressed in white, bareheaded, beneath a canopy carried by four of his newly invested knights, he emerged from the gates of his fortress to the sound of trumpets and the exultant boom of cannon. Behind him came his household: the Princes of the Blood, Peers, Judges and the Great Officers of State. The Queen followed, carried upon a gorgeous litter and attended by ladies of the court. She, too, was clothed in white. Thousands of people, from the greatest to the humblest, milled around them.

In honour of the great day, the filth had been scraped from the cobbles of the streets and each building the procession was to pass was freshly painted, gleaming with the gaudy colours and decorations usually to be found adorning the stands at jousting tournaments.

Similar scenes unfolded when Henry IV set out from the Tower in 1399. Six thousand horsemen rode with him. At the gates the Lord Mayor met the procession and led it through streets that still exist today. Down Cheapside and Fleet Street they marched in splendour; along the Strand, past the fine houses of the nobility; through Covent Garden (named after the convent of

The arches designed for the Mall by the Ministry of Works' Chief Architect, Eric Bedford, were an attempt to create decorations more distinctive and ambitious than the 'lines of washing' hung out to decorate the processional routes of past coronations.

Westminster) and the village of Cheeringe, now Charing Cross. Finally, they came to the Isle of Thorns, where Westminster Abbey stood. Along the route, colours blazed from walls, windows and gable ends, while the cheers of the onlooking crowds were lubricated by the torrents of free wine that flowed from the city's fountains, which had been specially converted for the day.

Livery companies vied with each other to display the most magnificent decorations and entertainments. Some erected triumphal arches; others hired tumblers and magicians to entertain both monarch and spectators. In 1547, Edward VI paused on his way to Westminster to watch an Aragonese tightrope walker teeter from the spire of St Paul's Cathedral to the Dean's Gate, and an 'angel' was lowered down to him from an arch in Cheapside. Edward's half-sister Mary I watched in amazement as a Dutchman scaled a ship's mast and performed death-defying acrobatics before perching astride the weathercock, 500 feet above.

Eric Bedford's approach in 1952 was more restrained, but no less memorable. Indeed, his free-standing arches in The Mall, built of tubular steel and adorned with lions, unicorns and crowns, are the enduring icons of the day. Forty years on, David Eccles pronounced them, 'the greatest single success in the aesthetic decoration of the Coronation'.

They seemed to symbolize the hopes of the new Elizabethan age, soaring elegantly towards the sky. But they looked so delicate on the drawing board that Bedford prudently decided to test one in advance. The experiment, conducted in Regent's Park, was a success and construction went ahead, although one of the arches did collapse while being erected over The Mall.

Decorating the flag poles between the arches proved less of a problem. After a weekend of intensive thought, Bedford triumphantly laid his design

LEFT: *Chairs for the Royal Dukes set out in the south transept of the Abbey. All the chairs and stools were specially made for the 1953 service and many were later bought by those who sat on them.*

for a banner and trumpet motif before the Minister, only to be told by David Eccles that he and his wife had come up with a similar idea which they had perfected at home with a broom and some pieces of paper.

This was far from being the only time that Mrs Eccles proved helpful to the Coronation design effort. She became Eric Bedford's unofficial assistant. All kinds of weird and wonderful duties were assigned to her. Notable among these was the ritual of holding an open umbrella inside Bedford's old car on rainy days. Its roof leaked so badly that without it they would have been soaked when they drove around to inspect the works.

The stands for the spectators inspired an innovatory portfolio of designs. Bedford had noticed in the film of the Coronation in 1937 that the spectators were so enclosed that they were sitting virtually in the dark. His sweeping cantilevered roofs, looking rather like half-opened tin-lids, allowed the people to see the Queen and the Queen to see her people. So successful was this design that modified versions of it can be still be seen in football grounds throughout the world. As a final touch, Bedford ordered the underside of each roof to be painted with heraldic symbols, thus adding more colour to the processional way.

BELOW: *The design of the Annexe attached to Westminster Abbey reflected Eric Bedford's wish to create a distinctive architectural style for the 'new Elizabethan age'.*

Stands were also needed for the Abbey, where the seating capacity had to be increased dramatically to accommodate not only all those entitled to be at the Coronation service but also the vast choir and orchestra that the occasion required. Once again, Bedford went to elaborate lengths to ensure that his designs would withstand almost any demand placed upon them.

Thus it was that a few weeks before the Coronation, Major Alan Dobson of the Grenadier Guards brought a detachment of some two hundred men to Westminster Abbey. Their task was to test the specially erected peers' balconies in full kit and heavy boots.

Dobson remembers that the building was still full of builders. They had been joined by a team of engineers who, with gauges and notebooks, were there to monitor the tests. Dobson stood below, on the spot reserved for the

ABOVE: *The verdict of the Trial of the Pyx is given in the presence of the Chancellor of the Exchequer. With Chancellor Norman Lamont in this photograph, taken in 1991, are Master Topley, the Queen's Remembrancer and Lord Adrian, then the Prime Warden of the Goldsmiths Company.*

Chair of Estate, and yelled orders above the din. On his command, the soldiers knelt, stood, sat down and shuffled around. They even simulated the moment when the peers raise their coronets and shout 'God Save the Queen!' Eric Bedford recalls seeing the steelwork flex violently but the stands withstood the soldiers' every assault.

Perhaps Bedford's most striking innovation was the design of the Annexe, a temporary building attached to the West Door of the Abbey. The procession has assembled there at every Coronation since the Coronation of William IV.

Once again, the Chief Architect was determined to improve upon the work of his predecessors in 1937. His solution was a building which, while reflecting the Gothic lines of the Abbey, was truly — and to some people, controversially — a product of the mid-twentieth century. One sign of the times was its entrance: transparent to allow the film and television cameras to show as much as possible of the Queen's arrival.

While there were no such elaborate plans to make in May 1992, the month did begin with a flurry of ceremonial activity. On 1 May, at Goldsmiths' Hall in the City of London, the analysts of the Goldsmiths Company had at last reached a verdict in the Trial of the Pyx. By ancient tradition, the Chancellor of the Exchequer, wearing a special robe, attends as Master of the Royal Mint to hear the result, which is read by the Clerk of the Goldsmiths Company in the Drawing Room. To the relief of the Mint employees, many of whom had made the long journey up to London from their factory in Wales, all the coins were perfect or fell within the 'Remedy' — the allowed margin of error. This was the signal for a celebratory drink, followed by lunch in the Hall.

Here, like his predecessors, Norman Lamont was called upon to speak and he took the favourable verdict as a cue to praise 'the high quality of the Mint's products and its worldwide reputation for excellence'.

The coinage of Britain and New Zealand and the jobs of the Mint's employees were safe for another year.

Meanwhile, at Wellington Barracks, across the road from Buckingham Palace, 2nd Lieutenant Justin Hunt-Davies was practising his Colour Drill. He had been chosen to carry the Colour at the Queen's Birthday Parade in June. Hunt-Davies knew he had a lot to learn. In the whole of his training at Sandhurst he had done, at most, an hour of Colour Drill, and now the Trooping the Colour was only a few weeks away.

You have to learn that everything is done at the same time as rifle drill, so you fit in with what the Guardsmen are doing with their rifles. It's all set movements. And, as you are in front of them, you can't see what they are doing, so you are listening to the sounds that they are making with their rifles, and, as a result, you obviously have to know rifle drill. There are different ways of carrying the Colour which you have to learn. And also, with royalty present, there are different ways of saluting with the Colour. And you have to learn the different ways of presenting arms to Her Majesty when you are going past her, both when you are marching in quick time and in slow time.

Although he practised with a broomstick, Justin knew that carrying the Colour would prove physically demanding:

Obviously I've got to build up the old muscles, shoulders and arms, because carrying the Colour for a long period of time, you have to carry it in a set position and it's very, very hard work.

With all the kit on, a bearskin and a tunic, which actually weighs quite a lot, you get very, very sweaty. So you do need to be quite fit before you start carrying the Colour.

Already, he had found there were countless other pitfalls:

You worry that your bearskin might fly off, or your swordbelt might break, so you spend hours rigorously checking your kit, even though it's probably in pristine condition, to make sure that nothing's going to fall apart.

I'm also very worried about dropping the Colour on some of the movements – that terrifies me! But I hope that with all the practice we're going to do, things will be all right on the day.

A few days later, at Westminster, the last in the long sequence of ceremonies sparked off by the General Election took place. Television has made the colourful and elaborate ritual of the State Opening of Parliament too familiar for it to need further recounting here.

But another ceremony that day is virtually unknown. While the Queen is at Westminster, a Member of Parliament is held hostage at Buckingham Palace against her safe return.

The hostage is always the Vice-Chamberlain of the Household, a political appointment held in 1992 by Sidney Chapman. While his fellow Members of Parliament listened to the Queen's speech at Westminster, he enjoyed the spectacle on television at Buckingham Palace.

The Imperial State Crown and other regalia are escorted into the Royal Gallery at the Houses of Parliament for the State Opening. It arrives and leaves separately from the Queen and receives equal ceremonial honours.

LEFT AND RIGHT: *Thanks to television, the State Opening of Parliament is now one of the best-known royal ceremonies. But behind the public spectacle, two further ceremonies make the State Opening possible. The Queen cannot go to Parliament unless the cellars have been searched beforehand: this is a throwback to the days of the Gunpowder Plot. Nor can she travel to Westminster unless a Member of Parliament is held at Buckingham Palace as a hostage against her safe return.*

June

The first day of June in 1952 found London in glorious sunshine. This weather was reflected in mood at Buckingham Palace where the official period of Court Mourning for King George VI came to an end that dawn. As the black edged writing paper was stored away, so the new Queen's reign came from behind the cloud of her Father's death. No longer did the courtiers don their black arm-bands or the royal ladies dress in traditional colours of black, purple and white. Once more, it was permissible to celebrate, attend private parties and be seen. The ceremonial calendar of June that year provided, as it always does, opportunities for the nation to celebrate its new beginning with confidence.

In 1651, just over three hundred years before, the reign of Charles II faced less hopeful omens. After defeat at the Battle of Worcester the King, fleeing from Cromwell's New Model Army, took shelter at Boscobel by hiding in an oak tree. Cromwell's Roundheads passed underneath the hidden king and thus Charles was saved the ignominious death by axe faced by his father. When Charles II was restored to his throne in 1660, he took trouble to reward the troops who had fought so loyally for his cause during the Civil War. Some years later he drew up plans for a hospital to care for maimed soldiers. It is thought that his sweetheart, Nell Gwynne, had given him the

BELOW: *Charles II hiding in the oak tree at Boscobel after the Battle of Worcester in 1651. His escape from the forces of Oliver Cromwell is recalled on Founder's Day at the Royal Hospital, Chelsea.*

idea, though this is probably the product of fanciful historians. The foundation stone for the Royal Hospital was laid in 1682 with the first veterans being admitted ten years later.

Traditionally, the Governor of the Royal Hospital waits until Christmas Day before announcing the identity of the inspecting officer at the forthcoming Founder's Parade. The In-Pensioners (so named to differentiate them from all other army pensioners) always hope that, if the Queen is not coming herself, she will be represented by a member of the Royal Family. However, this is not always the case. In 1952, Field Marshal Sir William Slim stood in for the new Queen and the parade coincided exactly with Oak-apple Day, on the 29 May. Ironically, many of the Chelsea Pensioners today, served with Lord Slim in the Forgotten Army of Southeast Asia and the Burma Star sits proudly among many medal rows. On Christmas Day in 1991, it was with great delight that the Royal Hospital heard that the Prince of Wales would take the salute in 1992, the tercentenary of those first arrivals at the hospital. It was especially significant as Founder's Day has been celebrated in every one of those three hundred years. News that he would be accompanied by the Princess of Wales further warmed the Christmas brandy.

The Royal Hospital is enormous, impressive and beautiful. It is set back from the River Thames with commanding views south across the river to Battersea, and north, to the King's Road. Charles II's magnificent statute by Grinling Gibbons (1648–1721) dominates Christopher Wren's Figure Court where the parade takes place. Despite the ravages of modern traffic, which flows unendingly all around the hospital grounds, the haven envisaged by Charles II for his ageing troops is still the peaceful and reflective place it was intended to be.

Early on the morning of 4 June, the day selected for Founder's Parade after the Chelsea Flower Show, the statue of Charles II was dressed with

branches of oak. This ritual commemorates the 'pious founder's' timely mode of escape from Cromwell's army and almost camouflages the bronze monarch out of sight. At the same time, baskets of oakleaf sprigs are taken to the longwards where about four hundred In-Pensioners are dressing for the ceremony.

Fixing his own leaf, while the preparations went on outside, was 100-year-old retired Battery Sergeant Nicholas Keating. He was about to take part in Founder's Day for the eighth time. As he put on his full-dress crimson coat and black tricorn hat, the uniform which has become such a feature of Chelsea Pensioners on London's streets and buses, his medals glinted with the memories of a military career which started during King Edward VII's reign in Pretoria, South Africa. Then, as the imperial eagles took the world to war in 1914, Sergeant Keating went to France with his artillery battery. He describes how it started:

Our first action after we got onto the battle front was at Ypres. We stopped there for three weeks, fighting day and night, day and night . . . until the end of November 1914.

The war progressed relentlessly and, at the Battle of Loos, Sergeant Keating won a Military Medal for running into no man's land, while under fire, to mend the broken cable of his Battery's field telephone. He served into World War II. In all, he had more than enough thoughts for an old soldier to savour on parade. With his back straight, his tummy showing the signs of good living and a determined gaze, Sergeant Keating left his small barrack-type room, descended the wide, shallow staircase and took his place in the ranks once more.

Eighty-five percent of us meet in the colonnade before the 'Fall-in'. Some of us haven't seen one another for weeks. We have a bit of a chat and a bit of a leg-pull here and there.

The Captains of Invalids bring the Pensioners onto parade at the latest possible moment. While these men are every bit the proud soldiers of their generation, gone is the ability to stand at attention for too long. Many In-Pensioners who can no longer stand on parade are seated under the colonnade, providing a proud line of scarlet to frame the main door.

The Prince and Princess of Wales' arrival was marked with a trumpet fanfare, the trumpet being the traditional instrument for drawing attention on the battlefields of history. It was sounded by military trumpeters from Kneller Hall, who stood precariously along the balcony. The wait was over for Sergeant Keating and the ceremony planned since Christmas could begin. 'Us little kids, we're all right,' he said, 'but these old chaps – their old knees are going!'

The ceremony is deliberately kept brief for very good reasons. The Prince and Princess inspected the line, talking to as many Pensioners as they could in the time available; both had a word with Sergeant Keating. The parading In-Pensioners then returned their compliment by marching past the Prince and the Founder's statue in a slow and dignified pace, to the tune, 'The Boys of the Old Brigade'. Sergeant Keating proudly recalled afterwards, 'I was the only one who stayed in step round that corner!'

As they passed His Royal Highness in two columns, half the Pensioners saluted with their left hands. This is the only time when the right hand is not used for a military salute. The purpose is to ensure that sight of the Inspecting Officer is not blighted by the hand. Also, in the days of tournaments, the knight's face could be seen more clearly by those watching the pageant.

The traditional cheer for 'our Pious Founder'.

After giving a resounding 'Three cheers for our Pious Founder', came probably the most important tradition of Founder's Day, as far as the In-Pensioners are concerned. As soon as the Inspecting Officer leaves, they are issued with their extra pint of beer. One pint has been on the daily ration card ever since 1692, which probably accounts for the proudly borne and affectionately described 'Chelsea chests'. The issue of the 301st extra pint on 4 June 1992 probably more than anything else christened the start of the next 300 years for this implacable band of distinguished old men.

Not far up the road from the Royal Hospital, at Wellington Barracks, a letter arrived for 2nd Lieutenant Justin Hunt-Davis. At the start of his military career Justin, aged 21, is 89 years younger than Sergeant Keating; to put this into perspective, there was still a year to go before World War I started when Sergeant Keating celebrated his coming of age. The letter was from Lieutenant Ben Stevens, the Ensign who had carried the Colour on the Queen's Birthday Parade in 1991. By tradition, the former Ensign writes a letter of encouragement to his successor. In its fraternal and jovial encouragement (the letter is largely unprintable!), one young officer passed his baton to the next. It came at a time when Justin found himself at the centre of considerable scrutiny in the lead up to the ceremony. The BBC wanted this, ITV wanted that; their interest evidence of the value Britain still places on this ceremony.

Probably more than any other annual ritual, Trooping the Colour has become the show-piece event to mark the passing of another year in the nation's life. In it, Justin's role is prominent. It also marks the Official Birthday of the Sovereign; the occasion for one of the two annual Honours Lists to be released and for Britons in the far flung embassies of the world to meet and drink to 'Blighty's' health.

The ceremony itself, for all the hype, is a private matter between the Queen and her Household troops. It has emerged through the evolution of

The Regimental Sergeant Major salutes the Colour before passing it to 2nd Lieutenant Justin Hunt-Davis. This is the only time a Warrant Officer draws his sword on parade.

For Justin Hunt-Davis, carrying the Colour was unforgettable. He described it as 'probably the most wonderful experience I think I have ever had. I was very, very privileged'.

a once vital military manoeuvre to ensure security in time of attack. When Charles II formalized the institution of the army, Colours were adopted by regiments as rallying points in battle. To some extent the Roman invaders brought the idea to Britain with their standards, which proudly bore the imperial eagle and the letters SPQR (*Senatus Populusque Romanus*). As with the Roman centurions, so British soldiers have adopted their Colours as an expression of morale, fraternity and, consequently, the regimental soul. Colours are, therefore, treated with considerable, almost irrational, respect.

Each evening of a military campaign was marked by a roll call before the Colour was Trooped through the ranks, to the sound of drums. This ensured that the troops recognized their Colour, knew who had it and where it would be kept during the night. Had the camp been attacked, every soldier would rally round the regiment's Colour.

The Foot Guards' regiments have been conducting this ritual in London since the early eighteenth century. The Changing of the Guard used to take place at Horse Guards and the Trooping process was considered necessary to ensure recognition, while music was used to communicate drill movements and other instructions to soldiers, many of whom were mercenaries and did not speak English.

The first royal birthday marked in this way was George II's in 1748; the parade was expanded but the purpose remained the same. Edward VII was the first monarch to attend regularly and the Queen took the salute for the first time on Thursday, 5 June 1952. It was the first great piece of pageantry she took part in after the King's funeral. She has attended forty Troops as Queen (the parade in 1955 being cancelled due to the national rail strike) and she seems to notice everything. Since 1959 it has always been held on a Saturday, in order not to disrupt the ever-increasing weekday traffic. The tribute paid to her by the Household Division is taken very personally by the Queen and, as he put on his tunic and bearskin, Justin Hunt-Davis could think of little else.

Wellington Barracks was full of activity on Saturday, 13 June. The air was pulsing to the sound of distant bands leading soldiers into place from barracks all round the capital; the sun, not always expected, was promising to raise the temperature for those on parade and the Officers' Mess dining-room was catering breakfast for the unending stream of officers arriving for the ceremony. Justin ate a good breakfast. He had been for a run with his soldiers at the break of dawn and knew that he needed plenty of energy to get him through the long-rehearsed parade.

At the end of the dining-room hung the Queen's Colour which Justin was to carry. It had been presented to the 1st Battalion Grenadier Guards by the Queen in May. A crimson silk banner edged with a gold fringe, it has the Union Flag in the hoist and, between yellow scrolls embroidered with the principal battle honours, is a bursting grenade. Before breakfast was over the Drummer arrived and, taking the Queen's Colour from the wall, folded it before putting on the long black leather cover. At the cover's head, an immaculately polished brass cone protects the lion and crown which surmount the pole.

Justin is 6ft 6in, which is tall by any standards; however, as a member of the Queen's Company, which was to provide the Escort to the Colour, his height barely reached the average. There is a measuring stick in the Company Office for testing recruits. There are no indications below 6 feet, instead a simple inscription which reads 'sorry' – the end of many a Grenadier's dreams.

Ever since Charles II made himself the Company Commander of the 1st Company, 1st Battalion, 1st Regiment of Foot, all successive Sovereigns have maintained this unique bond with this band of giants. Thus Justin's appointment had to be approved by the Queen; she knew something about him because Justin's father is Prince Philip's Assistant Private Secretary.

After a long drink of orange juice, Justin walked with another Officer through the park to Horse Guards Arch, where he put on the large white Colour Belt which instantly differentiates him from everyone else on parade. He recalls:

When we went up through St James's Park at the beginning I was nervous about the turn I had to do after he [the Regimental Sergeant Major] had given me the Colour, because I was very aware that that was the point of the Parade when I am the only person moving and all eyes were on me.

The music at the Queen's Birthday Parade recalls the days when the British Army included mercenaries, many of whom had a poor command of English. Orders were conveyed to them via the music.

Ben Steven's letter had mentioned the turn with a postscript that he shouldn't 'bob' when he did it 'even though 120 million people would have their eyes' firmly on Justin.

Queen Elizabeth, the Princess of Wales and young Prince Harry brought the first wave of anticipation to the spectators, the media and those on parade. But the Queen's arrival, timed to coincide exactly with the clock striking eleven o'clock and further marked by the distant thump of a 41-gun salute, had an effect in Horse Guards' Parade quite out of scale with the event and made the months of practice seem worthwhile.

Justin took the Colour from his Regimental Sergeant Major with confidence, turned to face the Queen's Company without fault and proudly absorbed the glare of eyes and cameras from around the world. All the rehearsals, which began in April, had paid off. He carried the Colour past the whole parade and lowered it in salute, as he slow marched in front of his Sovereign. 'I was nervous about the Colour getting wrapped up or of it not coming out of the Colour belt properly.' he says.

Meanwhile, at the other end of the country, 16 Phantom jets of 56 and 74 Squadrons at Wattisham in Suffolk stood silently on the baking tarmac, while their pilots take a final briefing. This was the last year of service for warplanes which had been part of the Royal Air Force's complement for 25 years. Their mission today was to pass in formation over Buckingham Palace at exactly one o'clock, in salute to Her Majesty The Queen.

Though only three were on Horse Guards, there are five regiments of Foot Guards; the Grenadier, Coldstream, Scots, Irish and Welsh Guards. Plumes and buttons mark their individual identity in uniform. In addition there are two regiments of Household Cavalry, the Life Guards and the Blues and Royals. The Cavalry brought the Queen's Birthday Parade to a close by trotting past, sending a turbid hazy dust into the air, which, with the heady smell of horses and their inevitable debris, left an impressive signature at the parade's conclusion. The Queen then led her troops home, with Justin close at her carriage's wheel.

Coming down The Mall and seeing the Queen . . . and Buckingham Palace in front of me and the Massed Bands was probably the most wonderful experience I think I have ever had. I was very, very, privileged.

But the day had hardly started for Justin and his soldiers. After all, they now had the Colour in their protection and must take over sentry duties at the London palaces. While he stood under the walls of Buckingham Palace, waiting to take up guard duty, there was a distant, threatening roar which seemed to grow with inexorable volume.

Those Phantoms had taken their cue and were approaching the Palace at 1000 feet and at 360 knots. The Queen and her family, joined by the Grand Duke of Luxembourg who is Colonel of the Irish Guards, were on the balcony in force.

The enormous and oppressive diamond of 16 Phantoms growled their swarm salute at exactly the time planned. As they veered out of London airspace, Heathrow, which has to suspend normal routines for this salute, resumed its role as the busiest airport in the world and Justin marched with

*Recognizing the Colour. The IXth
or East Norfolk Regiment of
Infantry knew which flag to rally
round in 1813.*

the New Guard to St James's Palace. His family joined him for a chilled glass
of something refreshing and lunch. Afterwards, everyone watched the video
to see dreaded moments repeated. Self-scrutiny is always the most acute
form of criticism. Meanwhile, like an echo of the past, the Queen's Colour
was propped in the corner of the room, the soul of a Battalion who have
added a new page to their history. In the Guardroom, Guardsmen not on
sentry were asleep. However, should anything have gone wrong, they knew
the identity and location of their Colour.

The Queen and her Court left Buckingham Palace for Windsor soon
after the Troop was over. The week ahead promised the pleasures of racing
at Royal Ascot, well known as the Queen's favourite relaxation. However,
before the horses reached the paddock, Her Majesty had an audience with
one of her former Prime Ministers.

When Edward III founded an order of chivalry in 1348, to reflect the
spirit of an England victorious over the French, he was on the one hand,
acting out his Arthurian dream of reinstituting the Round Table and on the

Edward III is said to have founded the Order of the Garter after the eponymous article of underpinning was dropped by Joan, Countess of Salisbury, at a ball in Calais.

other establishing a fraternity of loyal and proven knights to ensure their future obedience. The first Knights of the Garter encompassed the brave from Crécy and Calais, while including Edward's principal advisors and, not least, his son the Black Prince. The Garter has been used by successive Sovereigns as a means to reward, control, honour, bridle and flatter both Englishmen and foreign rulers. A walk through the Choir of St George's Chapel in Windsor Castle, looking at the brass stall plates which record almost all of the brotherhood, provides an *aide mémoire* to the great names which have shaped Britain. The Garter has encircled the leg of England's history and, to some extent still does. During the morning of 15 June 1992 the Long Walk of Windsor saw the arrival of today's Garter Ladies and

Knights. Among them three Prime Ministers, two Armed Service chiefs, three dukes, a Foreign Secretary, a Governor of the Bank of England and, showing a move to include women in this ancient order, one duchess.

They were gathering to hold a Chapter for the investiture of three new knights. Historically, meetings of the Order coincided with the Feast of St George, the Patron Saint of England. A medieval or Renaissance religious festival meant a period of fasting, prayer, thanksgiving, re-dedication and ended with a tremendous binge. Religious fervour has abated somewhat since the superstition and masochism of the Middle Ages. No longer must the Prince of Wales, Lord Longford and Lord (formerly Sir Harold) Wilson go off their food for a day or two in contemplation of God. The ceremonial today quite rightly reflects the dignity and beliefs of the 1990s clothed in the garb of a chivalric age.

The Queen was the last to process into the Garter Throne Room. The Chapter holds its conclaves in this panelled room dominated by swaggering paintings of royal knights swathed in their dark blue mantles with gold-lettered blue-velvet garters below their left knees. Behind the magnificent red throne canopy is a hidden projection room, for this room doubles up as the Queen's private cinema. With a royal instruction, two officers of the order by the titles Garter King of Arms and Black Rod, go to collect the three new knights. Sir Edward Heath, who served the Queen as her Prime Minister from 1970 to 1974 is the first, followed by the Lord Steward, Viscount Ridley, whose brother goes by the name of Nicholas, and the philanthropist and supermarket owner, Lord Sainsbury of Preston Candover, comes last. 'It means a great deal because it's not a political appointment', explains Sir Edward Heath. 'I've never received political honours and I didn't want political honours. But when the Queen herself says

BELOW: *Queen Victoria invests Napoleon III as a Knight of the Garter in April 1855.*

that she wants to confer the Garter upon me, then that's an entirely different category. That's why it means so much.' The Queen invests each Knight herself; first with the garter. While a young scarlet-coated page kneels in his breeches to hold the garter in place, the Lord Bishop of Winchester, who is Prelate of the Order, incants the prayers

To the honour of God Omnipotent, and in Memorial of the Blessed Martyr, SAINT GEORGE, tie about thy leg, for thy Renown, this Most Noble Garter; wear it as the symbol of the Most Illustrious Order never to be forgotten or laid aside, that hereby thou mayest be admonished to be courageous, and having undertaken a just war, into which thou shalt be engaged, thou mayest stand firm, valiantly fight, courageously and successfully conquer.

During the investiture with sash, star, mantle, collar, and George, the other Knights and Ladies of the Order, including the Royal Knights and Ladies sit in blue velvet chairs dressed in their own robes. The scene is medieval. The Queen's hat is busy with a cockade of ostrich feathers and, as she performs a similar task on each initiate Knight to the one Edward III enacted on the Black Prince, it was clear that, though everyone else needed to practice, she knows every move backwards. Sir Edward said:

When I was standing in front of the Queen I felt how important she is and the monarchy is to our country. She was symbolic of everything which had gone before, and she fulfills that purpose magnificently. So I couldn't help feeling at the time that this was for me a very humbling but at the same time honourable occasion.

1992 was the year of single market unity in Europe. However, on the 13 June at Windsor, a time of less easy continental relations was recalled. After a day's racing at Royal Ascot, the Queen and her family held a small private dinner party to which Valerian Wellesley, the 8th Duke of Wellington was invited. Military historians will quickly recall that the decisive battle of Waterloo was fought on 18 June 1815 and that the 1st

LEFT: *The Garter ceremonies of 1992 at which three new Knights, Lord Ridley, Lord Sainsbury and Sir Edward Heath joined the Order.*

RIGHT: *The Garter Knights process to St George's Chapel, Windsor for the Service of Installation and Thanksgiving.*

Duke's leadership delivered Europe from Napoleon's domination. But it was no casual interest in Waterloo which caused the Queen to include Wellington in the party. Rather, he was there to pay his rent.

British relief at Napoleon's defeat was ecstatic and, as the Duke puts it, his ancestor:

. . . at that time was regarded as saviour of the nation and indeed Europe. In 1816, by an Act of Parliament, a large sum of money, I think it was something like £600,000, was voted to buy a house and property for the first Duke.

After much consideration, Stratfield Saye House, in Hampshire, was purchased and developed to make it fit for the nation's new hero. The gift was magnificent and, though it did not quite reflect the donation of Blenheim Palace to the first Duke of Marlborough after his own defeat of the French, it provided a suitable seat for the Iron Duke. In return for the property, which the present Duke still occupies, a Quit Rent is paid to the Crown.

It was laid down by Act of Parliament that each year, the Duke of the day should hand to the Sovereign of the day a French tricolour as a Quit Rent for the property and that has happened ever since. I think in fact the actual ceremony of presentation is probably not a particularly old one. It may have happened once or twice in the last century, but I believe it was King George VI who actually restored the ceremony. Now it virtually happens every year unless for some reason or other it's inconvenient, in which case the flag is just handed in at Windsor Castle.

In commemoration of the victory at Waterloo, George IV ordered his architect to cover over a courtyard at Windsor and turn it into a great dining-room. The Waterloo Chamber, as it was called, is the usual location for this surrendering of rent. In 1952 the Queen received the tricolour here from the Duke's father on the same date, 18 June. At that great Waterloo Banquet all the Court and guests wore white tie and breeches. The late Duke of Wellington would have entered the Chamber under the portrait of his defiant forebear, he would have knelt before his young Sovereign and handed over the stave with its tricolour. Looking down from the walls are paintings of the victorious allies: George IV, Field Marshal Blucher, Tzar Alexander I and Pope Pius VII. In contrast, in 1992 the dinner took place in the Queen's private apartments; dinner jackets only were worn and there were no tiaras. While the style of things has changed in forty years, the tricolour and ceremony have not. The duke describes the tricolour:

It's a silk tricolour with gold embroidery round the edge and swags, I think you'd call them, hanging from the top. That part is the same each year. It differs only in that the date is put on in gold lettering on the corner of each flag.

Duly the tricolour was prepared for this year and the date 1992 was embroidered in the top hoist.

It's a symbolic ceremony to me; it's a very important historical link between the Duke of the day, myself for the time being, and my ancestor. It remembers an event

The Life Guards normally on horseback, march into position to line the route taken by the Sovereign at the Garter Service in St. George's Chapel, Windsor.

which took place nearly 180 odd years ago. I think it's a very interesting link with the past and it gives one the opportunity to register one's gratitude, as a family, for what the nation gave us in 1816.

We assemble before dinner and, once the Queen is there, a kneeling stool is placed in the middle of the room. I collect the flag, walk forward, stop in front of the kneeling stool, bow, kneel, hand the flag to the Queen, stand up, bow and walk backwards.

The result: another year paid for and no fear of the bailiffs. But what would happen if, for some reason, the Quit Rent was not paid?

I think we might find ourselves in a rather embarrassing position. At the end of each ceremony there are a few jokes about you're safe for another year 'cause you've paid your rent and so on but I don't think that it would be the serious intention of the Sovereign to remove the property. But it's a nice idea that we've got to pay it otherwise, you never know, we might lose it I suppose.

Every tricolour delivered to the Crown is kept in its possession. Although the 1972 flag hangs at Stratfield Saye, it remains the Queen's property. They are all kept in the Royal Library at Windsor. However, the new one is placed in the Guard Chamber of Windsor Castle over the Great Duke's marble bust. The Superintendent of the Castle, Major Eastwood, was handed the tricolour by the Queen. Immediately he walked the length of the Castle, through the now-gutted splendour of St George's Hall, and climbed a creaking step-ladder to remove the 1991 flag. In its place now hangs the 1992 tricolour and there it will stay until another year's rent is due.

July and August

Riverside British pubs provide an imperceptible quality to the nation's life. There can be few pleasures which exceed a hot sunny afternoon spent relaxing under a Thames-side weeping willow, with a pint of beer in one's hand looking across London's river. The drinker can watch the river traffic pass and enjoy the plentiful wildlife which lives along its banks. Chief among these inhabitants are the swans. In July, families of swans glide from bank to bank, while their young cygnets struggle to learn their graceful parents' style. Folk law from the Middle Ages tells us that these beautiful birds all belong to the Queen; just as Robin Hood knew, to his debt, that the deer of Sherwood Forest were owned by his King. Such royal patronage has ensured virtual protection for the sovereign of birds. However, on the River Thames, the Queen is not the only owner of swans. In the bleak days when their flesh supplemented a sparse winter's diet, there was great rivalry to claim ownership of swans from the Crown. Long since these dietary requirements have passed, the concept of ownership continues, is jealously guarded and was eccentrically maintained in 1992.

While duck, chicken and turkey regularly find themselves served up in the sandwiches of The Swan in Staines, the swans who swim on the

Stanley Spencer's painting of Swan Upping on the River Thames. Though the ceremony is still picturesque, today's scientists also take the opportunity to examine the health of the river's population of swans.

The skiffs corral the birds against the river bank. The cygnets can then be seized, marked and examined before being returned to the water.

river outside are left untouched. Well not quite. Any drinkers enjoying the traditional scene on Monday 20 July, during one of the few sunny lunchtimes of the season, while sitting out on The Swan's veranda, were witnesses to a ceremony of great history, extraordinary style and unquestioned scientific value.

Around the bend in the Thames came a small fleet of boats. The six skiffs which lead this Tudor progress are rowed by a hardy band of ageing rivermen, wearing a variety of bright, distinctive uniforms. The boats are low in the water, beautifully honed and varnished with bright painted banners fore and aft. Close examination reveals that there are three pairs; two represent the Worshipful Company of Vinters; two more, the worshipful Company of Dyers and the last two, Her Majesty the Queen, known in these circles as the Seigneur of the Swans.

This is the first day in a week of swan upping for these boats. After starting their river progress at Sunbury, The Swan at Staines provides the first stop for refreshment. Here Captain John Turk, the 78-year-old Keeper of the Queen's Swans, sits surrounded by a Court of Swan-Uppers. He is a distinguished-looking man in his scarlet coat, white trousers and nautical hat with The Queen's cypher embroidered above its peak. He sports a clipped, Edwardian beard as white as his laundered uniform. He took on the royal appointment from his father in 1963 (the Turks have been Thames Watermen since 1760) and consequently there is little he doesn't know about these graceful feathered creatures.

I thoroughly enjoy the whole thing. I have been Swan Keeper to the Queen for 30 years and was swan upping, oh, for 10 years before that at least. Swan upping means picking up all the newly hatched cygnets and marking them according to ownership. The Queen's swans, of course, are not marked at all; the Vintners' have a little nick on each side of the beak; and the Dyers', a little nick taken out of one side of the beak with a penknife. It's about the size and shape of a half moon of a fingernail. When the cygnet is young the lip of the beak is soft and gristly. We just take a little bit of that gristle out, without cutting into the bone of the beak. It's not painful at all and it doesn't do them any harm.

After lunch, the happy band resumed their hunt by taking to the river in their magnificent craft. The Queen's boats have enormous white flags with the royal cipher and crown in red and gold. John Turk sits in the stern of the senior boat and they head upstream. At each lock along the river's ascent, the crews make a special grog of milk and rum, which seems to do wonders for morale. No end of river boats join in the chase; most of them without a clue about the ancient ritual they are witnessing. Humorous ribald comments pass among the boats and it is a tremendous party.

Around another bend in the river, two cygnets are spotted with their parents. John Turk immediately takes charge and order springs from chaos.

We surround the swans with our six boats against the nearest bank to which they are swimming, and then we catch them with our bare hands. We pull them into the boats, smother the parents with our knees so that the wings don't flap too much because they are very dangerous; they've got a 6-foot wingspan and can fly at 40–60 miles per hour!! Then we tie them up and catch the cygnets after that. After examining the beaks of the parent birds to find out the markings on them, we mark the cygnets accordingly.

John Turk goes on to explain the modern application of this ancient practice.

Well, of course, it is only a traditional ceremony, but we do monitor the health of all the swans over the area of the Thames we cover in swan upping. After we have marked the cygnets, they are handed over to the Edward Grey Institute of Oxford's Zoological Department who measure, weigh and mark them; they take blood

In charge of Swan Upping in 1992, as in many years past, was Captain John Turk, the Keeper of the Queen's Swans.

samples and put rings on, so they know precisely where they were hatched and how they do in future years.

Some of the Edward Grey work at swan-upping ceremonies led to the ban on lead being used by fishermen in their tackle, because it was isolated as a cause of blood disease in the swans. Following this legislation, it seems the number of swans is increasing back to the river's old levels.

As the evening approached the river progress came close to Windsor, the Queen's ancient castle built to overlook the Thames and guard the surrounding area from attack. The landscaped river has fine views of the Sovereign's fortress, as the rowers pull the long strokes to Romney lock. It is time for the Swan-Uppers to remember the purpose and history behind their task and to reflect this in a ritual observance of the Queen's salute. John Turk describes why and how it is done.

We salute the Queen as Seigneur of the Swans. Two boats of the Vinters Company line one bank and two boats of the Dyers Company line the other bank. The Queen's boats just come up gently in between them. When they get abreast of each other, the companies' Swan-Uppers are ordered to toss oars, which means they stand up in their boats with an oar in each hand, pointing upwards. They have to give three cheers to Her Majesty The Queen and, as I am the Queen's representative on that occasion, I acknowledge that salute and instruct my Swan-Uppers to give a similar salute to the two companies.

As the first day ends, the skiffs pull into the Eton boat house and are lifted from the Thames by the Uppers. The storm clouds, which would be a feature of the rest of the swan-upping week, were gathering above Windsor's imposing towers and the river upstream could be seen flecked with hundreds of waiting swans.

In 1952, while the new Queen's swans were being upped for the first time in her reign, other, even more extraordinary aspects of her feudal inheritance were being decided. In a little-known building off Downing Street, the Court of Claims met in the Judicial Chamber of the Privy Council. There is no court higher in the land than the Privy Council and, because of our colonial history, it still meets to hear the appeals of capital convictions from some of the West Indian islands. The Court of Claims meets only at the accession of a new monarch and deals with applications from peers and bishops whose appointments or possessions entitle them to take part in the coronation.

Ever since William the Conqueror first sought to thank the Norman nobles who had made the 1066 Conquest possible, he devised a system of reward which carried certain conditions bonding the barons and their descendants to serving his Crown with loyalty. Some of the parcels of land he gave demanded in return that the recipient should carry out some mark of service at all future coronations. This process of feudal servitude was called Grand Sergeanty. What better occasion than the Coronation to remind the prosperous landlord that, despite his wealth, his first loyalty is to the monarch.

Records of the Court of Claims survive back to 1377, when John of Gaunt sat to consider the petitions of those seeking to attend his nephew, Richard II's coronation. Many of the petitions laid before the Court of Claims in 1952 concerned the direct descendants of those successful in 1377.

The new Queen's Court of Claims was chaired by her Lord Chancellor, Lord Simonds, and used its first of two sittings to declare what applications it would consider. The hearings were then posted for October. As the Queen had decided she would follow recent practice and not hold a coronation banquet, many of the more outlandish cases were outside their remit. For instance, rights to present a Messe of Dillegrout, a sort of uneatable potage of oats and barley, in service for the Manor of Addington; or the duty to provide napkins and linen, which was carried out by the Lord of Ashill as Royal Naperer and the Manor of Lyston's duty to make Wafers, presumably to take the taste of the dillegrout away, were all left in abeyance: and so the list goes on.

Perhaps the most magnificent service claimed is that of the Queen's Champion. William the Conqueror appointed Robert Marmion to be the first English Champion at the end of the eleventh century, and with it came the Manor of Scrivelsby in Lincolnshire. The estate has passed through the family, without upset, to the present owner, Colonel John Dymoke.

The owner of Scrivelsby is the Queen's Champion by virtue of the ownership of this land. My eldest son will inherit from me and that has applied back through the generations. I happen to be the 34th.

Up to George IV's coronation (1821), the Champion would have ridden into Westminster Hall on his charger and he would have challenged anyone who gainsaid the monarch's right to rule to a duel and, in doing this, he threw down his gauntlet three times and advanced up to the table where the Sovereign was banquetting.

When he got there, the Sovereign would drink his health from a gold cup. It would then be handed to the Champion who drank from it himself. He would

BELOW: *The Queen's Champion. At the Coronation in 1953, Captain John Dymoke was granted the right to carry the Union Standard.*

keep the cup, carrying it as he rode his steed out of Westminster Hall backwards. Not an easy thing, I can assure you, not that I've done that!

As a reward for doing this, he was able to keep the charger, which was the second best in the royal stables; the second best suit of armour, saddlery and the things that go with it; and also, of course, he kept the gold cup. So, he didn't do too badly.

But with no banquet planned for the Queen's Coronation, the young army Captain based in Egypt as Adjutant of his Battalion, knew there was little chance of throwing down his gauntlet this time. However, John Dymoke responded to the Court of Claims's request for petitions, as few had a greater or more romantic claim than he.

In 1952 we all knew there was going to be a Coronation so my trustee and I concocted a letter to the Earl Marshal, to be put before the Court of Claims, and I was granted the right to carry the Union Standard, so I was rather lucky.

Defending the Sovereign these days is no longer left to armoured Champions strutting about on horseback but to the men and women of the armed services. The army invests considerable effort in selecting and training the officers who will lead and administrate the business of combat in time of war. Likewise, those young men and women selected for training at the Royal Military Academy, Sandhurst put everything into achieving the Queen's Commission to command. No longer are these commissions bought from Parliament by inept younger sons, whose continued presence at home was starting to prove an aristocratic embarrassment.

The course at Sandhurst lasts a full year and, like the graduation ceremony of Universities, tradition recommends that those 'passing out' should do so with some style. On 7 August 1992, Sandhurst's Old Building parade ground was surrounded by stands. The parents who filled them, watched with pride as their sons and daughters marched as soldiers. Mr Wilson came down from Edinburgh to watch his son, Andrew, become commissioned.

Seeing him parading about, carrying on a great tradition, was to me the culmination of Andrew's dreams as a boy. He's really always wanted to join the army since he was in his early teens.

For all parents, it is the sight of their child slowly marching up the steps and through the vast black door of Sandhurst's grey frontage, that really makes them proud. During World War II, these cadets often marched on through the building, into lorries and off to join the great struggle. The tradition of playing the tune, 'Auld Lang Syne' is still used to guide the footsure cadets today. Andrew Wilson remembers:

I really wanted to get up the stairs as quickly as possible. A friend behind me knew fine well that I was trying to run up them! It brought together a whole year's training. We were following the footsteps of the great leaders of our past.

As I got through the door, a sigh of relief went through me and you have to contain your emotion until you get out of view from the spectators. After we got into the corridor, there was great shouting, hugs, clapping and everything was going up. Hats were in the air; people were stepping on each others boots to break up the hard work that had gone into them over the year.

The magnificent banquet held after the coronation of George IV. The King's Champion has entered on horseback. But all was not as it seemed: the Champion's charger had been hired from a circus and his suit of armour came from an antique shop.

We were all together, happy as could be, knowing fine well that this was our last day together.

The last person up the stairs is Major David Foster, Sandhurst's Adjutant. What makes his exit special is that he climbs the stairs seated in the saddle of his immaculate white charger, called Blitz. David Foster explains:

It goes back to 1927 when Captain Fredrick Browning was the Adjutant and there was a downpour on one of the rehearsals. He decided that everyone was to take cover, so he took his horse very quickly up the steps into the portico. It was considered to be such a spectacle that, from then on, the horse always goes up the steps.

Blitz has been doing this job for years now, he knows the parade almost better than I do. He's certainly able to anticipate going up the steps. He gets pretty excitable because he knows he always gets at least a packet and a half of Polo mints when he gets to the top.

I think it is a very significant moment as the doors slam behind me. It signifies the end of all the training and the young officers are very pleased; there are a lot of whoops and cheers and a few hats and that sort of thing, flying in the air.

Theoretically, as they pass through the door, each cadet becomes an officer. However, because administratively their commission runs from midnight, a new tribal ceremony has evolved to mark the magic hour.

Once all the uniforms of Sandhurst have been returned to the Quartermaster and, of course, any discrepancies have been paid for, the new officers put on their smart new Mess Kits. For Andrew Wilson, now a Second Lieutenant in one of the Scottish infantry regiments, his uniform consists of tight tartan trousers with a scarlet, blue-faced jacket.

Part of Sandhurst's magnificent grounds have been taken over with dodgems, roundabouts, discothèques, fly-walls, bucking-bronco machines and dancebands. As dusk falls, fleets of cars arrive; not parents this time but girlfriends, siblings and old school chums. The revelry is total; these new

The Queen at the Sovereign's Parade at Sandhurst.

Sandhurst cadets on the threshold of regimental life. Their training formally ends when they enter these portals.

officers have something to celebrate and nothing, not even a pair of tight trousers or spurs is going to stop them. As midnight approaches, the music is temporarily halted and everyone goes outside into the cool of a lakeside evening.

Most army officers wear their rank on shoulder epaulettes, typically it consists of a small, single star, or 'pip'. Until midnight, this remains covered for the ritual exposure, when the clock strikes and a massive firework starts a lavish display.

I wanted to be different. Many people had talked about tape and ribbon. I thought, well, it's a big night, let's go for it!! Let's do something unusual. So, I went shopping, purchased some cloth and humorous buttons and sat down late at night and sewed them on.

Officers and their friends gather tribally in groups; excitement has reached fever-pitch, helped by the music and alcohol of celebration. The clock is close to midnight now and girlfriends' fingers are poised to expose the epaulettes. Once again, Andrew had his own ideas. 'Right from the start I chose my sisters. There are no other closer people in my life and, when the fireworks are going each will reveal a pip.'

The clock strikes, the firework explodes and the commissions become real among tears, champagne, emotion and love. However, beneath all the revelry which this day's ceremony affords, is the very real task that will face these young men and women when the last dancing stops at dawn. For many, it will not be long before the streets of Ulster claim their professionalism; others will be posted to perform arduous tasks in the ever-increasing ambit of the United Nations and always there is the possibility of war. Whatever their allotted duties, these two ceremonies have done far more than a mere slap on the back and a piece of paper could have done. Apart from anything else, it has bonded family and friends in a young officer's achievement; their support may prove vital in the years ahead.

THE CEREMONIES
OF AUTUMN

The failure of the twentieth century democracies is in part attribut–
able to their failure to invest the state with ceremonial.

J.M. KEYNES *The Listener*, 26 August 1936

September

THE DOG days of the summer of 1992 were busier than usual at Buckingham Palace. The East Front, the imposing façade looking onto the Mall, designed by Edward Blore in the early years of Queen Victoria's reign, was being cleaned. Tarpaulins blanketed the towers of latticed scaffolding which branched out like jungle creeper across the face of the building as work progressed. The contractors were labouring against the clock: the job had to be completed by the time the Queen returned from holiday in Scotland in October.

Many members of the Queen's Household were on holiday, stalking the hills and moors of the Highlands or idling on the beaches of Devon or Cornwall with their families. Those who remained behind shivered in their offices as the freezing water used to wash the stonework poured down the windows.

Before she begins her summer holiday at Balmoral Castle, Aberdeenshire, the Queen inspects the guard which is stationed at the nearby town of Ballater for the duration.

They could at least contemplate a few weeks almost entirely free of ceremonies while the Royal Family paid their annual visit to their Scottish castle at Balmoral. A handful of formal events – a greeting by the Lord Provost, a brief stop to open a bridge or shopping mall, the inspection of the Royal Guard at the gates of Balmoral Castle – traditionally follow the Queen's arrival on board the Royal Yacht *Britannia* in Aberdeen harbour early in August after a cruise round the Western Isles. After that, apart from an appearance at the local Highland Games, the Braemar Gathering, the Queen can usually enjoy her holidays in private, in the knowledge that the most intricate rituals she may be asked to take part in are the Scottish reels at the Ghillies' Ball.

October

In the autumn of 1952, by contrast, there was no let-up for the organizers of the Coronation. On 31 October, the Court of Claims met for the second time at the offices of the Privy Council in Downing Street. In July, they had done little more than agree upon procedure: now they met in formal session to hear petitioners and judge the validity of their claims.

The hearing was held in the Council Chamber of the Judicial Committee in Downing Street. Two photographs taken at the time suggest that the Court presented a daunting prospect to any petitioner summoned to its presence. The panelled Council Chamber itself, designed by Sir John Soane in 1828, is spacious and sombre. Here appeals against decisions made by judges throughout the British Empire were decided: in the 1930s one

The Court of Claims in July 1952. The Duke of Norfolk (left), Lord Jowitt and Lord Goddard were among the members of the Court.

authority declared that, 'The sphere of jurisdiction of the Privy Council now embraces more than one-fourth part of the world.' Among the appeals heard by the judges were last-ditch attempts to save murderers from the gallows. Today, with the shrinking of the Commonwealth, its overseas' responsibilities are more limited, although domestic appeals from professional bodies such as the General Medical Council are still argued in this august room.

On 31 October 1952, a powerful group of men made up the Court of Claims. They included the Lord Chancellor, Lord Simonds, Lord Woolton, the Lord President of the Council, the Lord Chief Justices of England and Ireland and the Lord Justice General and President of the Court of Session in Scotland.

Twenty-one claims lay on the agenda. Fifteen of them had been 'allowed in whole or with reservations' at the last coronation in 1937. Among them, the Dean and Chapter of Westminster applied to 'instruct the Queen in the Rites and Ceremonies and to assist the Archbishop of Canterbury and to retain the Robes and Ornaments of the Coronation' in the vestry of the Abbey. The Bishops of Durham and of Bath and Wells asked to 'support Her Majesty at the Coronation, and to have certain privileges', and the Barons of the Cinque Ports (ports on the southeast coast) claimed their traditional privilege of carrying a canopy if used in the Procession in Westminster.

Not all these claims were allowed or clearly resolved. For example, Lord Hastings and Lord Churston both applied to carry the Great Spurs: the court decided that 'each of the claimants has established a claim to perform the service' and, 'that it be referred to the pleasure of Her Majesty to determine how such service should be performed'. In the end, they carried one each.

The Courts of Brotherhood and Guesting of the Cinque Ports meet to formulate an application to the Court of Claims in 1952. The Barons of the Cinque Ports successfully sought the right, granted by King John, to carry a canopy at the Coronation in Westminster Abbey.

These maple cups were designed for Mr Roy Boorman who, as owner of the Manor of Nether Bilsington in Kent, claimed the right to present them to the Queen. But the Court of Claims turned down his application on the grounds that this privilege had traditionally been exercised at the Coronation banquet. Since this no longer took place, neither could Mr Boorman's presentation.

The London and Fort George Land Company Limited fared less well. It had applied to provide a glove for the Queen to wear on her right hand during the Coronation service. The firm felt its claim was justified because it had bought the Manor of Worksop, a property whose owner had had the right to provide such a glove for generations: it was enshrined in the Manor's title deeds.

The Court's judgment on this claim shows that this application clearly worried those of its members who, as lawyers, were wary of setting precedents. However unlikely the possibility, the idea of a limited company making commercial capital out of its participation in a coronation was not to its taste. Thus, the London and Fort George Land Company's claim was dustily rejected on the grounds that 'the service claimed is one which by its nature cannot be performed by a limited company'. Instead, the Chancellor of the Duchy of Lancaster, Lord Woolton, was allowed to provide the glove.

The Duke of Somerset, who had asked to carry the Orb or a sceptre or to perform 'such other service or privilege as Her Majesty may be pleased to determine', received a terse rejection, as did one Prince O'Brien of Thomond who claimed the 'right to attend the Coronation Ceremony or alternatively the grace and favour of attending Her Majesty's Coronation, or to perform such other duty or privilege as may be decided.'

Perhaps the strangest claims came from a Mrs Mary Elizabeth Earle Long and a Kent businessman, Roy Boorman. Mrs Long wanted 'to carry the Queen's towel' and Mr Boorman asked permission to 'find for the Queen on the day of Her Majesty's Coronation . . . three Maple Cups and to present the same.' Both argued that the right to perform these services was laid down in the title deeds of properties they owned: Mrs Long was the proprietor of Heydon Hall in Norfolk and Mr Boorman the Manor of Nether Bilsington in Kent. Both applications were turned down.

THE CEREMONIES OF WINTER

The Monarchy of Great Britain represents the bonds of continuity of the nation – it is the link with the past, the security of the present, and the bridge to the future. Public ceremony is the extension of Monarchy, the constant reminder of its presence. . . . All of us can flock to the Changing of the Guard . . . and feel the presence of Royalty.

SENIOR ARMY OFFICER

November

WHEN THE Queen returned from Scotland in the autumn of 1992, she faced a round of State Visits and other diplomatic activity. Like the City Quit Rents, these have roots stretching back many centuries. In 1520, for example, King Henry VIII met the French king, Francis I, at the Field of the Cloth of Gold near Calais. The visit lasted for three weeks and was a spectacular display of wealth. The kings vied with each other in jousting tournaments and boasted about their possessions, but the event served its

The Queen and the Sultan of Brunei during his State Visit in 1992.

The Queen, with the Sultan of Brunei and his wife, the Raja Isteri. Behind the scenes at State Visits, there is scope for diplomatic and business initiatives.

purpose in repairing the often acrimonious relations between Britain and France.

State Visits are still used to mend fences. The Queen's visit to the newly united Germany in October provided one such opportunity, for she went to Dresden, the city bombed to destruction by the RAF during World War II.

At the beginning of November, the Queen herself played host to a distinguished foreign visitor, the Sultan of Brunei.

State Visits run to a timetable honed to perfection over the years. The man in charge at Buckingham Palace is Lieutenant Colonel Malcolm Ross. Ross begins discussions with the Foreign Office and the Visitor's officials months in advance, for, although the timetable seldom varies for the first two days of each visit, the later part of the programme is always designed to reflect the interests of the guest and his country. Just before the visit begins, a small gold-embossed booklet detailing the Ceremonial is printed and distributed to everyone involved. It is an impressive document, which lays out the timetable virtually minute by minute. Indeed, Ross says he 'plans every single second of every day of the State Visit.'

Thus, at precisely 11.30 on the morning of Tuesday, 3 November 1992, at London's Gatwick Airport, the doors of the Sultan of Brunei's aircraft opened to admit the High Commissioner for Brunei and his wife. Moments later, the Sultan himself came down the steps to be greeted by the Duke of York, local dignitaries and the Royal Household and Foreign Office staff who made up the British Suite attached to the Visitor's party for the duration. A Guard of Honour from the Royal Air Force stood by for inspection. In the past, the RAF flew an escort out to meet the incoming plane. The 'Top Gun' style aerobatics, a ceremony in themselves, must have been magnificent to watch and it is sad that this honour and display has ceased. Then the Sultan, the Duke of York and the Brunei and British Suites left Gatwick Airport Station on a crowded royal train for the 45-minute journey to

London. At Victoria Station, the routine is unvaried. The Queen and the Duke of Edinburgh were on the platform to greet their Visitor. With them were government ministers and the Chiefs of Staff of the Armed services. The Guard of Honour came from the Foot Guards. As the Sultan and his wife, the Raja Isteri, descended from the train, artillery salutes rang out from Green Park and the Tower of London, just as they have for centuries. Ten minutes later, the State Carriage Procession was underway. Victoria is almost next door to Buckingham Palace, so the route is a roundabout one, to allow as many people as possible to catch a glimpse of the Visitor with his

escort from the Household Cavalry. Of course most of the crowd gathered round the station are inconvenienced travellers, rather than a thrilled population delighting in a Sultan's visit.

At Buckingham Palace, the timetable is also well-established. Lunch is followed by an exchange of decorations and presents. The Queen invested the Sultan as a Knight Grand Cross of the Order of the Bath and gave him some eighteenth-century Chelsea porcelain. Her gift to the Raja Isteri was a silver cigarette box. In his turn, the Sultan presented the Queen with the Order of the Crown of Brunei Royal Family and a golden bowl and tongs made in his country. The Duke of Edinburgh received a ceremonial dagger, known as a Kris.

Later in the afternoon, the Sultan and the Raja Isteri paid the traditional visit to Westminster Abbey to lay a wreath on the Tomb of the Unknown Warrior. From there, they drove to St James's Palace where they were given an Address of Welcome by the Lord Mayor of Westminster. A charming and much-loved feature of every State visit then followed: tea with Queen Elizabeth the Queen Mother in Clarence House, reached by a connecting corridor from the Throne Room at St James's Palace where the Address of Welcome was delivered.

The State Banquet that evening was the proverbial glittering occasion with 170 guests. Although the opening moments and closing speeches are routinely made available to television, one strange throwback to earlier

BELOW: *Gerrit Houckgeest's picture of Charles I and Queen Henrietta Maria at dinner in 1635. Members of the Court watch from a balcony as their Sovereign eats.*

times goes unseen. High up on the wall of the Ballroom at Buckingham Palace, near the organ loft, is a wooden grille. Behind it is a balcony which, whenever State banquets are held, is thrown open to members of the Royal Household. Anyone, from the most junior secretary to the most senior official can apply for a ticket. Refreshments are served as the colourful scene unfolds below. While the onlookers could probably get a better view of the proceedings on television (although it is forbidden to photograph the Queen eating or at prayer), they are helping to perpetuate a long tradition.

In past centuries, courtiers clamoured to be allowed to watch their sovereign perform the most mundane of human activities, such as eating or getting up in the morning. This not only satisfied his subjects' curiosity, but also allowed the monarch to show off the perfection of his manners and the grandeur that surrounded him. A painting by Gerrit Houckgeest of Charles I dining with his Queen, Henrietta Maria, in 1635 vividly records this curious practice.

A State Funeral is seldom afforded to a commoner. However, no interment can have inspired quite as much emotion as the State Funeral held in Westminster Abbey on 11 November 1920. King George V was the Chief Mourner but no one knew who was being buried. The Unknown Warrior, a mutilated and unidentifiable corpse taken from the mud of a battlefield, could have been anyone. It was randomly selected by a desolate people to represent the greatest tragedy yet wrought by man.

Today, it is almost impossible to comprehend the impact of World War I on everyone alive at the time. It was the apocalyptic conclusion to the imperial tradition and the last great dynastic conflict. The Grim Reaper satiated his appetite by scything the lives of over one million souls. Some say that western civilization has never fully recovered from this slaughter. Death, particularly among the vitality of youth, became such a constant that the

The Queen leads the nation's tribute to the dead at the Cenotaph in London on Remembrance Sunday.

The Queen lays her own wreath at the Cenotaph.

British changed their reaction to it completely. The chivalric age had given life to a complex scheme of ceremonial to surround all obsequies; the Victorians had inherited this passion for mourning and, led by a widow Queen, developed it into an art. However, after 1918 little public display was made of grief and the stoic behaviour still encouraged today became vogue.

While private grief became more and more closeted, the nation reacted to the sacrifice in 1918 with an inspired and dramatic gesture of ceremonial solidarity. The generals had chosen to conclude hostilities formally at eleven o'clock on the eleventh day of the eleventh month. The annual act of Remembrance was marked, not celebrated, on the anniversary of this armistice. Each subsequent anniversary was observed with a two minute silence, which started punctually as church and market square clocks around the nation hammered out the memorial hour. Everything stopped. Cars and trains halted, radio stations fell silent and, through the ritual of ceremonial silence, the bruised Empire was joined in grief and rededication.

The forest of war memorials, lavishly erected across the globe in the 1920s, soon recalled their stone masons to inscribe a further half-million names after World War II. One girl, whose brother was killed in 1915, found herself focal to the Empire as it struggled to brave the renewed losses. As Queen Mother, she still appears every year beside Edward Lutyens' great Cenotaph on Whitehall for the annual Remembrance Sunday Parade in London. Her daughter, who played her part in 1945, now leads the national observance of the eleven o'clock silence.

On 8 November 1992, the Queen led the nation's tribute to the dead. At the same moment she and her family stood surrounded by politicians, servicemen, widows, widowers and clergy, every village in Britain met at its own memorial. There are no other great ceremonies that find such a spontaneous and complete echo. The blood-red poppies make their point and, despite murmurings that the practice is outdated, conflicts keep occurring to renew the meaning of sacrifice.

Perhaps this ceremony's greatest attribute is the excuse it provides for reflection, pride and reunion. People need a structure through which to express these feelings. Putting on campaign medals, service ties and berets to march with old comrades again, may seem bizarre but it is vital.

A single gun was fired to start the silence. Its shudder echoed wartime memories, shook birds from trees and lifted a skein of wildfowl from the lake in St James's Park. Two minutes of precious life filled with painful thoughts, before the second blast concluded the ritual ration of reflection. As the Queen laid her own wreath carefully on the Cenotaph steps, Sarajevo, the catalyst of the Great War, was ominously back in the news.

It was for that hard military life that Rifleman Prembahadur Rai left east Nepal to join the British Army in 1985 and it was to change the guard at Buckingham Palace that he sharpened his kukri knife in November 1992. The Gurkhas do not normally provide the Queen's Guard but, to enable the overstretched Guards regiments to train in their infantry role, other military units occasionally step into their ceremonial boots.

Prembahadur Rai comes from a noble warrior tradition, the Nepalese have provided regiments for the British and Indian armies for generations. In 1982, his regiment took their place in the Task Force to the South Atlantic. The approach of seven hundred Gurkhas, with their kukris flashing in the morning light, did a great deal to bring about an early end to the Argentinean occupation of the Falklands. The Grenadiers, who would soon be relieved by Prembahadur Rai's regiment, have also recently added new honour to their name in the dust of Iraq and Kuwait.

ABOVE: *The Remembrance Sunday Parade is a time of melancholy, reflection, pride and reunion.*

LEFT: *The Gurkhas change the guard at Buckingham Palace.*

The soldiers who change the guard outside Buckingham Palace are not actors put up for the tourists' amusement; they are all skilled infantry soldiers who stand ready to answer the nation's call in war. In guarding the Sovereign, they continue a tradition as old as kingship itself. Ever since men have selected leaders, there has been a need to protect them. The soldiers who stand guard over the Queen today inherit a tradition which certainly dates from the first piquet posted by William the Conqueror in 1066.

When Prembahadur Rai marched to the Palace on 25 November 1992 he was well prepared. First and foremost, he was a fully trained soldier, ready to do whatever is required to fulfil his task. In addition, for some weeks he had been learning how to stand on sentry, what to do if someone in the Royal Family arrived at or left the Palace and when to 'patrol'. Perhaps the most surprising lesson was how to recognize members of the British Royal Family. All the Palace Guardrooms have boards covered in photographs of the Royal Family; this makes it easier to recognize the Queen's lesser-known relations, like the Duchess of Gloucester, or Princess Michael of Kent, for instance. In training at their camp at Church Crookham, the Gurkhas used back copies of *Hello!* magazine to improve their recognition of a Royal Family very different from their own in Nepal.

Standing at attention, to await the Gurkhas' arrival, was Major Tim Reeve, a Grenadier and the Captain of the Old Guard. That morning he completed his duties after 48 hours on guard. Behind him stood the immaculate ranks of Grenadier Guardsmen, to whom the sound of the approaching band heralds the chance to get off duty and out on the town. The falling rain did little to dim their enthusiasm. In Tim's pocket was an old lockless key. It was made by Chubb, and has a simple Crown at one end with a set of worn lock-teeth at the other. This is the symbol which sets the hand-over process in motion.

The Grenadier and Gurkha Ensigns patrol across the front of Buckingham Palace while the band plays incidental music behind. Meanwhile the sentry boxes and Guardroom are handed over.

With a flourish of Light Infantry bugles and style, the Gurkhas take position facing the Grenadiers, in front of the Palace. They swing their SA80 assault rifles in salute to each other and the Old and New Guard Commanders start their business. Tim Reeve explains:

Having saluted each other, we march onto the middle of the Forecourt and I hand over the key and that starts the ceremony rolling.

The key represents control of the guard of the royal palaces and, as I hand it over to the New Guard Commander, it shows to him that he is now in control and responsible for that guard.

There are four sentry boxes at the front of Buckingham Palace. When the Queen is at home these are all manned; if she is away, two are left vacant. These boxes used to be located outside the railings, until the pressure of tourism forced them inside. Observant visitors will still find the special paving stones where once the sentries used to march their 15 paces away from and back to the sentry box.

Once the two Guard Commanders have symbolically exchanged the key, a flourish of activity begins. Prembahadur Rai goes with a small detachment to the Guardroom at Buckingham Palace to prepare for his first sentry duty; he will be posted in front of the Palace to relieve a dismounting Grenadier. At the same time, Corporals from both Old and New Guards inspect all the sentry boxes, to ensure they are clean and tidy. Meanwhile, the officers pace the length of the Palace in pairs, patrolling. Tim Reeve explains:

At Waterloo the officers would patrol up and down in front of the squares formed by the men, both to show that they were present and in control, and also to keep themselves moving, so that they wouldn't be shot at by French sharpshooters.

The only sharpshooters around these days are the hundreds, often thousands of tourists who make this daily pageantry a pilgrimage of their visit to Britain. The birth of the railway, while Queen Victoria was resident at Buckingham Palace, introduced the capital city to tourism. Air travel has made international tourism an ever-more popular pursuit and, with its history legitimized by a living and continuing monarchy, Great Britain stands out as a spectacular destination. Unlike Vienna, which can boast plenty of great buildings and artefacts, London still has a sovereign to wear its Crown Jewels, a monarch to occupy its palace and royal guards that change daily outside its gates.

On the day the Gurkhas took over at Buckingham Palace, the railings were plastered with their daily crowd of tourists. Taxis were coming and going to deliver group after group of anoraked and camera-carrying sightseers. For most, the sound of the bands and a film-spool or two shot off at the passing soldiers is enough to satisfy an appetite for London's pageantry. With little to explain what is going on, the ceremonial often appears confusing, if not boring. It seems the soldiers arrive, stand still for a considerable time without doing much and then leave.

While the music plays to the crowds, Prembahadur Rai has a few moments respite in the Guardroom away from the public gaze. His Sergeant checks him over. This includes an inspection of the kukri.

BELOW: *The symbolic key, representing control of the guard of the royal palaces, which the Old Guard hands to the New Guard during the ceremony.*

The kukri is our traditional weapon. We have been using it for a long time. Normally we carry it in both war and peace-time. We use the kukri in war as a last resort for self-defence and, if we have the kukri we feel stronger, we use it very effectively!

Not only the black polished scabbard and the brass hilt are checked: 'My superior takes the kukri and he scrapes his nails.' They are so sharp that, even a light brush against the thumb nail produces a powdered shaving. After the inspection is finished and the knife is back in its ever-ready place, the Corporal marches the first relief out to take over their sentry duties. Prembahadur Rai recounts:

This is my first time I'm doing Public Duties. My responsibilities as a sentry are to assist the police in protecting the Queen, the Palace and saluting the members of Royal Families and also VIPs coming in and leaving. When I am posted in the sentry box, the Corporal reads the order to me – either my responsibilities or the paces for patrolling that I should take to my left and right.

While the orders are read to him, Prembahadur Rai stands next to the Grenadier Guardsman about to be relieved. The size difference is enormous. The Guardsman is already more than 6 feet high and, with his tall Bearskin hat, seems like a giant beside the powerful but slight figure of Prembahadur Rai. As soon as he finishes reading the instructions, the Corporal shouts the most significant order of the ceremony. 'Sentries PASS!'

In one slick movement, the Guardsman marches away and Prembahadur Rai steps into his place. Thus, ceremonially and symbolically, taking over the responsibilities. This is the stuff of changing the guard, though most of its witnesses miss this subtle moment.

Once all the sentries have been replaced by Gurkhas and the Guardrooms become filled with the delicious smell of 'Bhat' (the famous Nepalese curry), the Old Guard leaves and the Forecourt of the Palace becomes deserted once more.

ABOVE: *The Grenadiers hand over to the Gurkhas on the forecourt of Buckingham Palace.*

RIGHT: *Before Prembahadur Rai mounts guard, his corporal must first check that the sentry boxes are in good order.*

December

December brings the promise of Christmas magic. In the middle of recession, the season of goodwill was badly needed in 1992. Everywhere preparations for the great festival got underway. Children put Advent calendars on their walls to count away the days. Carol singers wander rural lanes and rustic villages, singing for charity and eating mince pies. Cribs are carefully taken from tissue-paper boxes and laid out once more, to underline the poverty of Christ's birth. With precarious diplomacy, each family steps its way through their individual traditions, without which 'Christmas would not be the same'. In this land of the 'Green Man', Celtic habits die hard as houses are decorated with holly, ivy, trees and mistletoe. Indeed, ritual superstitions in our blood unknowingly emerge at Christmastime.

The churches struggle to keep the mystery of Christ's birth alive in the minds of their congregations. Thus the town of Glastonbury, deep in Somerset, plays its part in trying to keep the heavenly message of goodwill alive Every Advent it sends the Queen a very special Christmas present.

Glastonbury's Christian lineage predates Saint Augustine. Close to the local church of St John the Baptist, are the ruins of Glastonbury Abbey, once the wealthiest monastery in England, until Henry VIII had it destroyed in the Pilgrimage of Grace. The massive remaining foundations and pillars give a clue, both to the breathtaking size of the church and the importance of Glastonbury in England's spiritual history. The Tor, whose mystical cone-like form dominates the skyline above the town, was a place of spiritual importance in the earliest times. Endless legends sprang up to bolster that importance and, thereby, fill its coffers with pilgrims' money. For instance, the Abbey claimed to be the resting place for King Arthur's remains.

William Blake's portrayal of Glastonbury's most illustrious visitor, Joseph of Arimathea.

The original Glastonbury Thorn.
Today's trees have been grown from
cuttings taken from it.

Countless pilgrims came to visit his royal grave. Perhaps it was this financial incentive that provided Glastonbury with the legends around its Holy Thorn. The Reverend Patrick Riley's wife, Elizabeth, explains:

The legend has it that when Joseph of Arimathea is reputed to have come to this country, possibly with some of Jesus's disciples, he planted his staff in the ground and it sprouted and grew into a tree. And there's still rather an elderly small tree [on Wearyall Hill] and cuttings have been taken from it ever since. There's one in the churchyard, one in the Abbey and others around the town. They all flower at Christmas time.

Joseph of Arimathea was Christ's secret disciple who took his master down from the cross and placed him in his own tomb. Supposedly he travelled to Somerset in 63AD to bring the gospel to Britain. The legend says that, when Joseph arrived at Glastonbury to build his church, the pagan locals were sceptical. He prayed for a miracle. According to one account:

Fixing his pilgrim's staff in the ground, it was no sooner set in the earth but just like Aaron's rod it was presently turned into a blossoming tree, which supernatural miracle made numerous spectators, who came to see the wonder, be very attentive to hear his preaching the Gospel.

One thing is certain, the thorn is not native to England. However, it grows plentifully in Palestine. While this does not confirm Joseph's travel arrangements, it provides a strong botanical link with the Holy Land. In the Middle Ages, a hawthorn bursting into white flower at Christmas must have seemed an annual miracle in itself. Elizabeth Riley feels its symbolic importance today.

I think the Glastonbury Thorn is a special tree because it shows the continuity of Christian life in this town, from those early days, nearly two thousand years ago, when followers of Jesus Christ came here. It's a holy place and that continuity is shown in the flowering of the tree, year by year.

The Thorn (*crataegus oxyacantha praecox*) blossoms twice a year – the second flowering being at Easter, after which the tree bears a crop of red berries. It produces clusters of small white flowers, flecked with pink. In 1992, the mild winter weather meant that, on 16 December, when the Mayor and two small children took cuttings for the Queen and Queen Mother, the Thorn was bright with blossom. Elizabeth Riley describes the ritual:

Outside the church is a large grassy area with the tree in it and we assemble the school round two sides of the grass. Proceeding from the church comes the Mayor, other dignitaries and the clergy from all the churches in Glastonbury.

They meet on the grass and my husband encourages the children to be still and quiet, while we remember the presence of Our Lord Jesus Christ. He goes on to explain the legends and traditions of the Holy Thorn. After that, the two eldest children in the school are invited to come and cut sprigs of the Holy Thorn, to send to Her Majesty the Queen.

My duties on the day are to bring a basket and secateurs and hand them to the Town Clerk.

A rickety aluminium ladder is set beside the tree and Patrick Riley guides the young children as they clip carefully with the secateurs. The little churchyard is packed with children, parents, shoppers and visitors swept into this private town ritual. There are about ten cameramen and two news crews. Sadly, with so much ill in the news, everyone knows that this bit of Christmas spirit is unlikely to catch the news editor's eye. Then the Mayor steps forward in red robes and a black tricorn hat and the press reel off their pictures.

Schoolchildren traditionally cut the sprigs of thorn which are sent to the Queen and the Queen Mother.

The tradition of sending the Holy Thorn to the Sovereign each year was re-established by Patrick's forbear, the Reverend Lionel Lewis in 1929. The custom is believed to predate the Reformation. The Thorn's legend had spread throughout a land conscious of holy relics and religious magic. All medieval monarchs, like their people, were superstitious and spiritual; a gift of Holy Thorn, with all its implications, would have been highly prized. Small posies of flowers were often sent with petitions to great men, to sweeten their response. The Abbey sent a gift of Holy Thorn to Thomas Cromwell, Henry VIII's Vicar General, in a bid to persuade him that complaints about the behaviour of monks were unfounded. It stalled dissolution but not for long. James I and Queen Anne were happy to part with quite large amounts of money to gain a cutting, even though the spiritual significance had been whittled away.

Elizabeth Riley continues:

After the ceremony, I pack up the parcels and take them to the Post Office. I just love to think of this expression of loyalty and, particularly this year, of love and devotion to the Royal Family.

Glastonbury has got such an ancient history and the continuity between the past and present is so important; it's one more demonstration of the continuity of our Christian heritage.

Back in the Church, Elizabeth is surrounded by children who watch, fascinated, as the boxes are packed. She explains each step, as the children ask about the Queen, Christmas, and the Holy Thorn. Copious quantities of tissue paper protect the sprigs and wet cotton wool provides sustenance. Finally, after reading out the letter Her Majesty will soon read, Elizabeth seals it into the box and the package addressed to H.M. THE QUEEN, BUCK-INGHAM PALACE. She comments, 'I don't have to put a stamp on these parcels. I just hand them straight over to the counter clerk.'

At eleven o'clock the following day, the Queen's Page placed the sprigs into a vase, put the letter onto a silver salver and walked quietly into the Audience Room, where Her Majesty The Queen was working at her desk. He placed it on the desk, 'The Glastonbury Thorn, Your Majesty.' Elizabeth Riley continues: 'It is precious to me to think of the Queen placing the Holy Thorn on her writing desk and, when I watch her at three o'clock on Christmas Day, I always look to see if it might be displayed on her writing desk as she speaks to us.'

Shortly before ten o'clock, on Friday 18 December, Yeoman Gaoler John Maher struck a match and lit the candle in the Tower of London's lantern. The light flickered and caught its reflection in the polished buttons and scarlet cloth of the uniform watchcoat he was wearing. He blew out the match and placed it in an ashtray on the table beside his black velvet Tudor bonnet. As he shut the lantern's door he checked his watch, there were a few minutes to go. The fortress had been closed to the public for a few hours now, so all was quiet. Quiet enough to hear his colleague lead the evening's posse of ticket holders in to witness the oldest military ceremony in the world. With one minute to go, he took the hat and placed it squarely on his head. He strikes a determined military appearance which is enhanced by an immaculate white beard; he is the stuff of London's postcards. The moment arrives: he takes a firm grasp of the lantern and picks up the massive jangling set of Queen Elizabeth's Keys. He explains:

The ceremony begins at precisely seven minutes to ten, when I leave the Byward Tower carrying the lantern and the Queen's Keys. I go to the Bloody Tower and hand the lantern to the unarmed soldier, who carries it throughout the ceremony. I then 'fall in' between the two lead escorts. The Sergeant, who commands the whole escort, 'steps off' the party and we march to the Middle Tower.

In order to understand why John Maher needs such an elaborate and well-armed military escort, we need to forget the way the Tower looks today and imagine it in the thirteenth century. In those days, when the gates were opened each morning, the whole of Water Lane would fill with traders and stalls; there would be bartering, shouting and no end of squealing market animals. The newly cobbled street laid in 1992 would then have been feet thick in farmyard filth; the stench would have been unimaginable and the atmosphere unsafe and unlawful. John Maher elaborates:

Remember, this place was built by a conquering king in the heart of a hostile and resentful population. Officials were treated with the gravest of suspicion and were often violently assaulted when they left the safety of the precinct of this place. The Chief Warder, who is responsible for locking and securing the Tower each night, was so violently assaulted on one occasion that he was in fear of his life and the safety of the keys of the Tower of London. He demanded of the Governor on that night that he be provided with an escort from the military garrison that has always been stationed here. The Ceremony of the Keys tonight derives from that demand made all those hundreds of years ago.

ABOVE: *Yeoman Gaoler John Maher takes the leading role in the Ceremony of the Keys at the Tower of London.*

As the Escort took Yeoman Gaoler John Maher along Water Lane, the small crowd of guests stood with their backs to the fearful river entrance known as Traitor's Gate. John's forebear in office would have stood here to receive Cardinal Wolsey, Archbishop Cranmer and Thomas More, to name but a few, and place them in the awful custody of a fortress few traitors ever left alive. By comparison, as the military party marches to the outer gate, sounds of their footsteps are drowned by the sirens of modern 'gaolers' going about their business outside the walls. John points out:

The ceremony is, of course, by no means an entertainment. It is an ancient and historic military ceremony that has taken place here at the Tower of London every night, without fail for the past seven hundred years.

It is perhaps interesting to note that not even Hitler's blitz of the capital city halted the ritual.

There have been no State prisoners incarcerated in the Tower since Josef Jacobs was shot by firing squad in 1941. It might seem that undue trouble is therefore being taken in the daily ritual of bolting the Tower gates. However, this ancient building contains something of considerable intrinsic value. Edward III moved his royal regalia here from Westminster for safe keeping in 1327, a year before his coronation. Today deep in a sealed vault, secured by enormous safe doors are the Crown Jewels of Great Britain. They are the symbols of monarchy and stand for the nature of constitutional government that the British people have chosen. Quite apart from their ancient symbolic importance, the Regalia contains some of the most famous and valuable gem stones in the world. These jewels are the principle reason why William the Conqueror's Tower is the most popular tourist attraction in London. Such notoriety has its risks. The British Crown Jewels would be a valuable prize for any robber. It has happened before as the Yeoman Gaoler explains:

Somebody did once attempt to steal the Crown Jewels. A fellow called Colonel Blood made friends with the Keeper of the Crown Jewels, a man called Talbot Edwards. He came to the Tower to visit Edwards and so assaulted him that he subsequently died of his injuries.

The Regalia was taken, squashed into bags and hidden under long coats as Blood and his accomplices rushed to escape with their prize.

The robbery went wrong because Talbot Edwards' son, who was returning to the Tower with an Escort, heard the hue-and-cry that was going on and captured them.

There is great suspicion as to the reason an attempt was made to steal them, because King Charles promoted Blood, gave him a pension and, I think, an estate in Ireland.

John Maher's escort would be perfectly equipped to deal with any latter-day 'Colonel Bloods'. While the Ceremony of the Keys goes on, there are a number of Guardsmen patrolling the area where the Regalia is kept. These soldiers are armed and dressed in combat clothing. Intricate plans have been drawn up to deal with any possible attack on the crypt-like bunker, deep beneath the Jewel House. The securing of the old gates each evening by

Today, the lantern carried during the Ceremony of the Keys adds to the atmosphere. Originally, it was used to help the Yeomen Warders find the keyholes in the dark.

Yeomen Warders, in the light of a lantern, is a symbolic display of the real military might available to protect St Edward's Crown, the Sceptre, Orb, Ampulla and Spoon.

Once the Middle Tower has been secured, the great bolts pulled across and the locks turned, the escort brings John Maher to the inner gate, under the Byward Tower.

The escort 'presents arms' as myself and the Watchman of the night swing the gates closed. We have to be very careful because they are very old, a little warped and they don't match. Once we've got them secured in position, we then put the huge hasp into place; it's put into the lock, which is many hundreds of years old, which is then locked and secured.

There's no point coming back tonight to pick the lock because the keyholes are only on the insides of our doors.

Standing beside the two Warders is the Lantern carrier.

Yes, the lantern these days is probably purely ceremonial but, remember, before these jolly nice electric lights, we would have needed that lantern in these dark recesses to have seen the keyholes.

Both gates are now closed securely, so the Sergeant marches the Yeoman Gaoler back to the Bloody Tower. As they get close, the sentry, who has been standing still throughout the locking process, steps out of the shadows. 'Halt', he shouts, with his rifle aimed directly at the approaching escort. Bearing in mind what this dark alley must have been like in the early centuries of this ritual, especially when the river fogs hung heavy around the Tower's turrets, it is easy to understand why this sentry needs to check the identity of the approaching footsteps.

Like any body of men meeting an armed challenge the Sergeant does what he is told. John Maher describes the exchange of words: "Who comes there?", to which we reply, "The Keys"; "Who's keys?" and again we reply, "Queen Elizabeth's Keys".'

That is enough for the sentry, who comes out of the challenge, shouts, 'Pass Queen Elizabeth's Keys and all's well!', and salutes as the escort marches by, under the Bloody Tower. It is sobering to think that this ceremony would have taken place the night the young Princes were supposedly smothered to death in the Bloody Tower; that Sir Thomas More would have watched the escort pass by from the slit window of his cell and that Queen Anne Boleyn would have heard the challenge in the last wretched days of her life, as the scaffold was built for her beheading on Tower Green.

Under the soaring edifice of the White Tower, the whole Guard have 'turned out' on the Broad Steps to honour the keys. The Sergeant halts before them at a few seconds to ten o'clock. In the presence of the Queen's Keys, all the soldiers 'present arms', and, with typical ceremonial timing, the clock strikes the hour at the precise moment John Maher steps forward to pronounce the prayer, 'God preserve Queen Elizabeth!' and the soldiers respond with a loud, echoing 'AMEN!'.

John takes the keys and lantern to the Governor for safe keeping, while the Bugler sounds the Last Post. Then the soldiers melt up the steps to assume the night's duties. The Watchman turns to the visitors lucky enough to witness the latest observance of the oldest military ceremony in the world and asks them the age-old question, 'So, it's all locked up, how are you going to get out of the Tower then?' It does not seem to worry them unduly but, when they do finally walk from the Tower's mystery and safety, back into London's streets, some probably wish they had their own escort. After seven hundred years, the dangers of walking about in the darkened alleys of London are still as real as they were when villains first attacked the Chief Warder in the thirteenth century.

At three o'clock in the afternoon on Christmas Day, the Queen broadcasts to the Commonwealth. She has done this every year since 1952, except in 1969. As the Queen's reign has witnessed some of the most enormous advances in media technology, she has been quick to respond and alter the format of the broadcast accordingly. While there is no ceremonial associated with this annual event, it has become a significant ritual in British life. Most homes find five minutes in the hectic day to silence the over-

BELOW: *The captivating mixture of ancient and modern in the Ceremony of the Keys has ensured its survival. When it is over, the Tower is guarded by regular soldiers.*

excited children and listen to the Sovereign. Traditionally the Queen picks a theme which underlines the Christmas message. When it is broadcast throughout the Commonwealth, it symbolically brings the family of nations together.

The western churches believe that the Magi, or 'three kings from the east' who came to worship Jesus, arrived in Nazareth twelve days after his birth. Their arrival and the presentation of princely gifts has been marked as the Feast of the Epiphany. The Epiphany, or manifestation of Christ, was the first evidence to the world that this baby was indeed the son of God; after all, if a maternity ward in the Midlands was suddenly visited by two Presidents and the Emperor of Japan, who lavished valuable presents on the alarmed parents, this would be noticed and have a significant effect on the world's media.

All Christian monarchs saw the humility of the three kings as an example. They should do likewise, in gratitude to the God by whose grace they rule. English kings made Epiphany a Coronamenta, or 'crown-wearing' and went in state to deliver their gifts of a 'Byzantine' (a gold coin), frankincense and myrrh. George III was the last monarch to go in person. Ever since, two of the Gentlemen Ushers have represented the Sovereign. This year, one of the two was Major Nigel Chamberlayne-Macdonald. He described the event:

There are ten Gentlemen Ushers in all. One of the two selected for the Epiphany must wear spurs. We represent the Queen and deliver the gold, frankincense and myrrh to the Altar of the Chapel Royal in St James's Palace, on two silver-gilt salvers.

I carried the gold this time and Captain Michael Fulford-Dobson brought the powdered frankincense and myrrh. The door opens and we march in, bowing to the Altar three times as we approach. The aisle in the tiny chapel is lined by the Yeomen of the Guard. Holbein's ceiling is over our heads. The altar is dressed with all the Chapel Royal's plate. It all looks wonderful and the music sounds glorious.

There are 25 gold coins delivered and a representative sum of money is distributed, on behalf of the Queen, to elderly people associated with the Chapel Royal. The frankincense, which comes from the Boswellia Sacra trees of Hadhramaut in the Yemen, is given to churches which still use it during their services.

The Sub-Dean takes the gold from me and it is placed on the altar. We go to sit in the Royal Pew, take Communion and listen to the music. But, when the service ends, the ceremony isn't quite over. You see I'm wearing spurs and there's a rule against that!

James I made the rule in 1622, though the ban had been in existence before. He decreed that, 'No man whatsoever presume to wayte upon us to the Chappel in bootes and spurs.' The choristers were encouraged to keep a look out for culprits. Anyone they found would be fined 'Spur Money'. It became difficult to keep the choristers' concentration as they were so eager to boost their purse. The Dean of the Chapel Royal issued a further edict, with the King's approval later in 1622.

If anie Knight or other person entituled to wear spurs, enter ye Chappell in that guise, he shall pay to ye quiristers ye accustomed fine: but if he command ye youngest quirister to repeat his 'gamut' and he faile in ye so doing, the said Knight or other, shall not pay ye fine.

The gamut, comes from the words *gamma* and *ut* which preceded the Latin song of musical notes in the scale. Julie Andrews taught the von Trapp family a similar gamut in 'The Sound of Music.' These days, *ut* has been replaced by 'do' and is followed by re, me fa, so, la, te and do again. 'Do, a deer; re, a drop of golden sun', etc. When Major Macdonald came down from the Royal Pew the Sub-Dean took him to one side and asked, 'Sir, a Child of the Chapel royal desires the honour of addressing you.'

The Major replied, 'Certainly.'

Then the Chorister made his point, 'Sir, I perceive the wearing of spurs within Her Majesty's Chapel Royal, and I therefore beg to request the payment of the customary Spur Money due thereon.'

Realizing that he is in a bit of a corner here, the Major remembers that there is still a way out, 'Boy, before acceding to your request, I require you to repeat the gamut.'

But on 6 January 1993, Major Macdonald was not as lucky as the 1st Duke of Wellington in 1851. The Iron Duke had challenged the chorister to recite but the boy failed and went without his bonus. But Major Macdonald was willing the young lad on.

I tried not to look too fierce as the chorister challenged me. He recited the gamut perfectly, so I gave him the crisp new fiver and congratulated him. I don't know how much he got to keep for himself.

Nothing misses the effects of inflation, when the fine was imposed it amounted to one penny.

THE SUPREME CEREMONY: THE CORONATION

I thought, I'm having a marvellous dream. There were all those people in their beautiful clothes, the music out of this world, and the principal characters moving with supernatural dignity. Well, they were watching a fairy story, and a real one, not just make-believe. You see, men and women, they need food to eat and water to drink, but their imaginations are also desperately hungry for fairy stories. And this was one, where Church and State were working together, weaving the fabric of a single dream.

DAVID ECCLES, Minister of Works and Coronation Organizer

JUST BEFORE Christmas 1992, six aristocratic ladies gathered in the Throne Room at Buckingham Palace to have tea with the Queen. For the first time in forty years, the Coronation Maids of Honour were to be reunited with the Sovereign whose train they had carried at the Coronation. Back in 1952, the Earl Marshal, the man in charge of this greatest of all royal ceremonies, had chosen the girls carefully. They were all

Forty years on: the Maids of Honour reunited in 1992. Left to right: Lady Moyra Campbell, Lady Rosemary Muir, Lady Glenconner, Lady Willoughby d'Eresby, Lady Rayne and Lady Mary Russell.

daughters of noblemen. Two were tall, two were of medium height, two were petite. All would look beautiful and elegant in the fabulous gowns created for them by the court couturier Norman Hartnell when they shared the limelight of the Coronation service with their Queen. And so it proved, as the group taken by society photographer Cecil Beaton in the Throne Room on the afternoon of Coronation Day shows.

In 1992, as the ladies waited to meet the Queen, all talk was of that momentous day four decades before. Lady Moyra Campbell, the daughter of the Marquess of Hamilton, had travelled to London especially for the reunion. She said of her role in the Coronation:

It was one of the most thrilling experiences of a lifetime, really. It's very hard to put into words what one felt: enormously honoured, very very grateful and tremendously exhilarated and thrilled.

Lady Rayne, born Lady Jane Vane-Tempest-Stewart, the eldest daughter of the eighth Marquess of Londonderry, remembered her amazement at receiving her invitation to take part:

The letter came through the post and I just couldn't believe it. I had to sit down on the bed and look at it again, because it just came like a bolt out of the blue. I had no preparation or warning for it. And of course one was filled with great elation and great pride really that one had been chosen.

For the reunion, the dress worn by the Queen on Coronation Day had been brought to the Throne Room from its store in Kensington Palace. The Queen remembered how she had worn it on a Commonwealth tour after the Coronation. Though designed for a British summer, it had proved stiflingly hot in the tropical heat of Ceylon.

The Maids of Honour had found their own gowns difficult to wear, according to Lady Mary Russell, daughter of the Earl of Haddington:

The gowns we wore were very pretty. The embroidery on them was absolutely stunningly beautiful with the thistle and the rose and the Welsh emblem, but they were not comfortable. They were very tight and they were rather crackly – that's the only word I can use to describe it. They were tight under the arms and, well, it was a bit like being in a suit of armour, slightly prickly.

Yet to the millions who watched the Coronation in black and white on television, on the streets of London as the processions wound by, or from privileged seats in the Abbey, if ever there was a Day of Majesty, this was it.

Isobel MacConnell was one of the thousands who camped out on the pavements on the night before the Coronation. To a girl in her twenties, the celebrations brought a touch of magic to a London still steeped in post-war austerity:

It really was fairyland suddenly. From being very grey and a rather depressed city, suddenly there was a completely different atmosphere. People were more cheerful, and there was this extraordinary feeling that you were going to a party. Of course this was heightened by the wonderful decorations which were everywhere and the crowns which seemed to float in the air above your head as you went. It really didn't matter that the weather was pretty awful because you had all this to look at, and it did lift people's spirits immensely. You felt something new was about to happen and there was a feeling that youth was really going to try and do something worthwhile for the country.

Preparations for the Coronation gathered momentum in the last weeks of 1952. At dawn one November morning, a cavalcade moved off from Buckingham Palace. Its task was to check the route that the Coronation processions would follow: no traffic islands or other obstacles could be allowed to impede the pageant.

In December, the nave of Westminster Abbey was closed so that construction work could begin on the stands for the spectators and the 'theatre' in which the Queen would be crowned. The transepts and sanctuary were kept open for services over Christmas, and then the whole building was turned over to the Minister of Works, David Eccles, and his ministry. David Eccles recalls:

The Dean and Chapter have by tradition to hand it over to the Minister of Works. They give me the keys and everything and off they go. And they don't go back inside for nine months. We had a tremendous amount of material to get. It's quite a long way from the West Door to the Altar, so we built a little railway and the material was sent up the railway, and we had to build stands. I think more than seven thousand people got into the Abbey, more than ever before.

And, of course, besides those stands, we had to build the places for the cameras, and we had to change the lighting altogether. We also had to do a lot of rather ordinary practical things. You had to have a sufficient number of places where people could retire to, if they felt they wanted to. And there were all the service books and each person had to have a special chair.

The St Edward's Chair was restored by scientists and art historians before the Coronation.

We had a good team. The thing is that if you can make people feel that they are engaged in something which really matters, and it's a little bit beyond ordinary daily life, then they'll work for you day and night!

Algy Greaves, Canons' Verger of the Abbey, remembers the upheaval:

After Christmas in 1953, the whole of the Abbey was closed to the public until the next September. And what happened then had to be seen to be believed, because in came the Ministry of Works which almost completely took over the place. They not only cleared the chairs out, they cleared us out too. Then all these hundreds of chairs had to be stored away wherever they went.

After that, in came contractors. You've never seen anything like it: huge planks, girders and everything were brought in. There was even a railway running up the nave of the Abbey, over David Livingstone's grave, which I rather stupidly called Livingstone Junction, which didn't help that much. But it looked more like a dock-yard than the Abbey, and gradually all these planks and girders and things were built up on either side of the nave and also in the transepts where of course the people sat.

As it got nearer to the Coronation, I nearly got sent to the Tower one day, because somebody came in and they said what did I think it looked like? And I said Drury Lane Theatre, which wasn't perhaps the best sort of description. But the next day there was a small headline in the newspaper, "Verger said, 'Abbey looks like Drury Lane'." Now I didn't mean this in a facetious sort of way, but with all these galleries and all the drapery, it did look rather theatrical, in fact. It didn't much look like Westminster Abbey.

At the Earl Marshal's headquarters in Belgrave Square, John Brooke-Little had been hard at work for months:

There was an awful lot to do, because, after all, there hadn't been a coronation of a married sovereign since Queen Anne. There weren't many precedents from Queen Anne's coronation – the record is very thin indeed – so we had to start again.

We had such things as television to cope with, and the whole Abbey has to be turned into a sort of theatre. In fact, the centre of the Abbey is known as the Theatre on this occasion. Then hundreds of people had to be sorted out. Making the lists of guests was very difficult and we had to take the Queen's wishes on every-thing that we did. And sometimes things didn't work out and one had to do it again, and there was everything to rehearse. So it did take a long time.

The staging of the ceremony was plotted out on an enormous great chart on the wall. Every participating person had a pin, with a different colour for peers, a different colour for pages, a different colour for heralds and so on. Each pin had their name on it. And these were moved around so that we could see which was probably the best position to put people in, because we didn't start rehearsing of course until towards the end.

For John Brooke-Little and his colleagues, there were some distractions from the daily grind:

We had a lot of curious enquiries. The press office of course dealt with some. Some of the written enquires, though, and the oddities, came to us, and we had a special policeman for the lunatics. He was a large and jolly man, and he used to come once a week and I would go through the strange letters with him.

We got quite a lot of people claiming to be the King of England. That was a fairly common letter: you didn't pay much attention to those.

Some of them were funnier. There was one written on about fifteen sheets of lavatory paper which came from a would-be King, and it was written in pencil. He put on the bottom, 'Pardon common paper, but have no money.' So he'd actually have done very well if he had become King!

At the Royal School of Needlework, embroiderers worked against the clock to sew the Queen's Coronation robes. To this day, the School ensures that the necessary skills are readily available by including the sewing of Coronation robes in its permanent curriculum. 19-year-old Monica Neal was one of the small team in 1953. The wheat and olives design was kept top-secret:

We would be working in this little room, all on our own together, the whole lot of us, just the people who had been chosen. We had police guards outside. It was very very secret. We weren't allowed to talk to newspapers or anybody.

We all had to work very, very hard. There were, I think, five people on either side of it at that time, all the time, Sundays, Saturdays, the whole time.

We were all working to the very end and we got to the last pieces that were being done and it was decided that everyone with the School would come and put a stitch in. So it was all covered up so that nobody could see the design, and we would pre-

Sewing the Coronation robes at the Royal School of Needlework. The design was so secret that a policeman kept watch outside the door.

pare a piece of gold threaded up and each person would come and put a stitch in from cleaners to kitchen staff. Everyone – men and odd-job men, would come and put a stitch in and we were very happy to do that.

As June approached, rehearsals began. With five other sailors, Leading Seaman William Davies was drafted to a platoon which would have to spend up to eight hours standing still, lining the processional route:

We did ten days' training at Chatham Barracks. They'd recalled pensioners, Gunner's Mates that had served in the war. They trained us to a very high standard of squad and rifle drill and also told us the necessary details to stop you fainting. The thing is, you have to curl your toes and that stops you falling over.

One day we had a full dress rehearsal where we spent eight hours lining the road-ways of Chatham Barracks. We were the street-lining party in our position with rifles. Other men were assigned to march around with poles. On the pole was a placard, and on the placard would be chalked 'Duke of Westminster', 'The Queen' or the various dignitaries that would be taking part in the Coronation.

And along came old Jack-Me-Hearty plodding along the roadway: 'I am the Duke of Windsor' or 'I am the Duke of Westminster', then your officer would recognize that this man required a general salute or a butt salute given with the rifle. Slope, arms, present arms, whichever salute was warranted at the particular time. So that when we went to the Coronation on the actual day, the officer knew, 'Here's the Duke of Westminster coming, we'll give him a butt salute. Oh, here comes the Queen, we'll give her a good'un!' and up would go the rifles for 'Royal salute, present arms!'

The Earl Marshal, mindful of all the disasters at previous Coronation services, insisted upon intensive rehearsals at Westminster Abbey. Everybody was required to attend, except the Queen. At her husband's request, Lavinia, Duchess of Norfolk stood in for her:

We took a house in London. I had to be ready to come to the Abbey every single morning at about half-past nine or ten o'clock.

I suppose I took part in a rehearsal every day for six weeks, and the Queen only came to the dress rehearsal.

The Duchess was happy to help her beloved husband in this way:

He did everything by instinct. He had no education, so it was all instinct. He knew exactly what to do. It was most interesting to see him with all these people who were twenty or thirty years older than him. He knew exactly what to tell them, what they had to do. Sometimes, they were rather amazed that this young boy should be telling them what to do.

The Queen leaves Westminster Abbey with the Duke and Duchess of Norfolk after a rehearsal.

CORONATION OF HER MAJESTY
QUEEN ELIZABETH II

By Command of The Queen

the Earl Marshal is directed to invite

to be present at the Abbey Church of
Westminster on the 2nd day of June 1953

Norfolk.
Earl Marshal

As a result of her long stint at rehearsals, the Duchess is the only person alive, apart from the Queen herself, and the Queen Mother, who has actually been crowned in Westminster Abbey:

The crown itself was very heavy, and one had to make sure that it fitted absolutely right. It feels like falling off the whole time, so you have to tell whoever's putting it on to put it on a little bit forward or a little bit back.

It was very awe-inspiring, really. It was wonderful. You had to be very careful that you carried everything right, and that you walked straight and that you felt quite safe with it all on you.

Paul Scott, one of the choirboys, also remembers a demanding rehearsal schedule:

You had to attend a number of compulsory rehearsals. These were held at St Margaret's, Westminster. You had to attend eight of those rehearsals and for each of them you had to have a coloured stamp on a card. It was reputed that, had you missed any one of those rehearsals, you would not have been allowed to be in the Abbey on Coronation Day. They gave us a ticket which had a tear-off strip for the two dress rehearsals in Westminster Abbey, and if you attended those two dress rehearsals you were finally given your pass for entrance to the Abbey on Coronation Day.

The six Maids of Honour also worked hard, as Lady Mary Russell remembers:

We did train like Guardsmen, really, I mean we were taken through from starting just by ourselves and then gradually being introduced into the Abbey, into the whole setting, and then with all the other people involved, until the whole came together.

Just before the Coronation, they rehearsed with the Queen herself in Buckingham Palace. 'I remember she was wearing a mock train,' says Lady Mary Russell. 'I think it was made of some kind of stiff material. Of course is was cut to exactly the right length and shape so that we were in the exact positions we would be in, and we paraded up and down the passage.'

The Queen walked more quickly than the Duchess of Norfolk, but the Maids of Honour found few problems and considerable amusement in the run-up to the big day.

'I remember one day,' says Lady Rayne, 'when the Archbishop was trying to show us something we had done wrong. He was trying to show us how we should walk down the stairs. He picked up his cassock, walked down, and then tripped and literally rolled over and over about three or four times. He skipped about two steps and of course we all burst out into giggles and actually he did, too. He got up laughing, so that's what broke the tension a bit.'

There were parties all over the capital that night. In their tens of thousands, people from all over Britain and the world had arrived hoping to find a good vantage point from which to watch the processions. In Piccadilly Circus, the crowd passed the time by dancing a conga. A square-dance suddenly engulfed Regent Street. Beneath the illuminated decorations, old songs floated in the night air. Rain fell spasmodically, but no one got soaked, many taking refuge in makeshift tarpaulin tents which sprouted notices like 'Lover's Nest' and 'No Vacancies'.

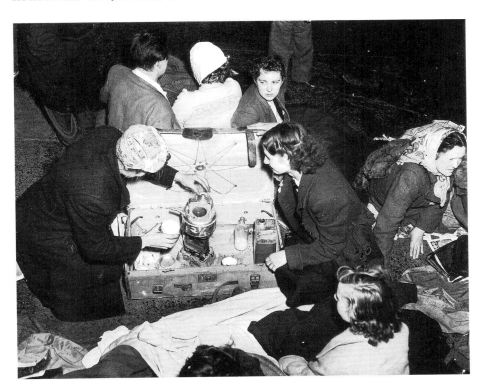

The appropriately named Joyes family cook breakfast in Trafalgar Square on Coronation Day.

Ray and Maureen Raper of Gosforth spent their wedding night amidst the Coronation crowds. They had managed to get a hotel room for their honeymoon, but the urge to join the crowds was irresistible, as Maureen Raper remembers:

It was so exciting to be on the streets of London. We changed from our going-away clothes into street clothes and went out into the streets. We found a position just outside Buckingham Palace at the end of Birdcage Walk.

There were masses of people there of all nationalities and all age-groups. We wanted to get a front-line view of the Coronation.

We danced and sang, and everybody was very good-natured. Very quickly, when it started to get dark at night, people started eating chestnuts and hot sausages and there was a smell of sizzling bacon pervading around the streets of London, and wine glasses clinking. There was generally a very happy atmosphere, and it was very memorable.

Ray recalls what happened when the people around them realized they were newly-weds:

We did make friends with a number of people, particularly a young Indian couple. They said, 'Oh, these people are just married!' So everybody said 'Oh, congratulations', and they got out, as if by magic, bottles of whisky and sherry and goodness knows what. We had a whale of a time, quite honestly. It was great.

We didn't care about the weather, we didn't care about the rain or anything. We just enjoyed ourselves. We were there to enjoy ourselves. We had had what people might say was the happiest day of our lives because it was our wedding day, and we were just full of exaltation, full of happiness, both for ourselves and for the Queen.

The Times described the scene.

It was a cosmopolitan crowd. Opposite the Cenotaph an American announced proudly that he had hitch-hiked by air from San Francisco. With equal pride his neighbour claimed 50 years in Walthamstow. In the Mall sailors from Ceylon looked for a last-minute place. Some Canadians bivouacked in the Haymarket. A Rhodesian settled down beside them.

In towns of tents throughout the London parks, the troops drafted in to line the streets or march in the procession snatched a short night's sleep, their training done. Some like Leading Seaman William Davies found themselves in a very strange billet: the deep air raid shelter beneath Clapham Common.

To reach it we entered an entrance two hundred feet above us and down into this dark and dismal hole we came. But when you realize these probably saved the lives of thousands of Londoners during the Blitz in the war, one night on these was no hardship to us, really.

They gave us a 'donkey's breakfast', which, in case you don't know, is a palliasse filled with straw, and a blanket. To us it was a refuge. We were tired, we were wet, and it was a place to get our head down and we did.

No one had any inclination to disobey the rather curious order that had been posted during training:

In the days before 2 June, London's children found there was nowhere to play: the parks had become camps for the troops taking part in the Coronation.

On the noticeboard one morning there appeared a notice signed by the Commodore but written by God knows who. And it said that all ratings – not officers, mind – all ratings must not indulge in sexual intercourse or over-indulgence of alcohol forty-eight hours prior to the Coronation. Whether this would affect our standing or not, I don't know. But when you realize that the only women in the barracks were Wrens on duty and they were all gone by six o'clock, so all you had were about 1600 men! So to say it was a peculiar notice, it definitely was.

As dawn broke, the four hundred Gold Stick officers on ushing duties in the Abbey were already in place. Soon after five, the lights went on all over Buckingham Palace. In the first light of the morning, Isobel MacConnell saw a strange sight:

We heard first of all this incredible sound of what sounded like a very heavy body of people marching. And through the mist, because it was extremely misty and it was beginning to rain quite heavily, came these blue-coated figures of policemen, all marching through with very measured tread, coming through from the tube station.

They'd come from all over the Southern Counties and it was almost eerie because they swung by in the gloom. Then I turned to follow them and they'd opened the gates of the park and there were the newsboys. They were selling the first editions and I had got some money with me, so I bought one of everything and took them back.

We shared them out among all of us and the one that we had most difficulty with was the one that was printed in gold because we hadn't enough light to read it in the dawn.

And in the papers was headlined that news that Hillary had conquered Everest and the New Zealanders in the crowd nearly went mad. It was a wonderful moment.

In Kensington Gardens, the mind of RAF man Neil Thornton was not on Mount Everest but another battle for survival. He and fifteen thousand other servicemen had been living eight to a tent for ten days:

One of the big problems was, of course, washing. Trying to supply any form of water for approximately fifteen thousand people was of course very difficult, and it meant that you either had to shave in cold water or wash in cold water. But fortunately just outside the entrance to Kensington Gardens there was a public convenience and wash and brush up.

At seven o'clock in the morning we used to troop down in our overalls with towels round our necks, holding our soap and razors and that. We used to queue up on the pavement just to get this hot water. A normal wash would take just a few minutes, but by the time you'd queued up you might be there an hour or an hour-and-a-half.

BELOW: The Queen left Buckingham Palace shortly before 10.30 a.m. and did not return home until the afternoon.

The Gold State Coach was built for George III in 1762. It was decorated by an Italian artist, Giovanni Battista.

The writer Naomi Mitchison was also up early. She had a seat in the Abbey. She thought that both the men and the women looked strange in their formal Coronation–wear. She herself, she wrote that afternoon, 'looked, in my lace, like some quite nice but funny character. Mrs Tiggywinkle perhaps.' She went on:

But gradually one warmed up, beginning to feel that one was part of some genuine Occasion.

The women at least began to hold their heads up; most of the men were either awkward in fancy dress or firmly subfusc, as though about to pass an adult 'exam'. This impression increased with the appearance of the Vice-Chancellor of Oxford in lovely scarlet and mauve – but, I'm sorry to say, smoking a cigarette in academic dress. Men look well in robes, except when the modern trouser leg insists on peep– ing through, but ordinary court dress seems rather silly with the so obviously unused and unusable sword. Privy Councillors looked nice – behind me one gasped, 'I'll have to undo the neck soon.' – and so does the Navy: most men are the better for epaulets.

Outside, the crowds waiting for the procession found plenty to amuse them, as Isobel MacConnell remembers:

We weren't prepared for the fact that a lot of the guests that were going to the Abbey were going to find it easier to walk down the Mall to get to the Abbey, and, poor things, they got cheered because we were rehearsing our cheers. So every– thing that came down got cheered and you could see an eminent couple coming along – she in her fur coat over her finery and he all wrapped up in a great coat because it was very, very cold, and they were walking along quite happily until the first burst of cheers came out. Then they put their heads down and they scuttled. And then of course there was the inevitable dog. I don't know where dogs come from on processional routes, but inevitably there was a dog and it got cheered. It, too, scuttled.

One of the Maids of Honour, Lady Rosemary Muir, daughter of the Duke of Marlborough, was impressed by the jollity of the crowds she saw as she rode to the Abbey in a coach. They had not allowed the appalling weather to distract them from the celebrations:

They were all highly excited and waving. I think that they had been entertained by various bands and things during the early hours of the morning. Everyone was very good-humoured and very excited. There was a very festive air, and it was a very exciting atmosphere certainly.

The Times correspondent described the procession:

Just before 9 a.m. approaching cheers were heard, and the Lord Mayor's coach came in sight. From that moment onwards, the cheers came in waves, reaching fortissimo as well known figures passed by, until a thunder of loyalty and affection greeted the arrival of the Queen in her State Coach, to be doubled and redoubled as successive stands caught sight of her gracious smile, and felt for a moment the radiant presence of the Sovereign. The Earl Marshal stood forward on the steps of the annexe to receive her, and as the Queen was escorted within, her personal standard was broken on the mast above the cupola. . . .

Then the Queen came, a young and gracious figure, with her hands clasped motionless in front of her and with a smile to acknowledge the homage of curtsies and bows. She walked lightly and in slow state, her head held high, and passed, the complete Queen, to her consecration.

Hour by hour the scene of ordered preparation within the abbey had grown in beauty and solemnity. Now it was almost complete. Beneath the high tranquillity of the sweeping arches of the great church tiered wooden galleries, faced with figured cloth of blue and gold, were filled with a brilliant company; and colour from nave, choir and transepts came no longer in scattered notes but in thronging chords.

Lady Jane Willoughby, now Lady Willoughby d'Eresby, was overcome by the glory of the moment:

I had never taken part in a major religious ceremony like this. And there was this terrific burst of music echoing round the Abbey as we first came in, and there was the feeling of being part of a religious sacrament, part of history.

When Henry III rebuilt the Abbey in 1220, he planned that it should out-do Rheims in France as the most magnificent coronation church in the world. The whole scheme aimed to achieve two things: firstly, it would provide at its crossing a wide and open setting for the supreme act of coronation and, secondly, it would have at its centre the shrine of Saint Edward the Confessor. The Saxon king, whose canonization had brought dignity and legitimacy to the English crown, would bring sanctity to the anointing and crowning to his successors. When the Abbey was completed, some two hundred years later, the vast darkened and empty church would have been lit by a glow of golden light. This translucence came from behind the High Altar, where the opulent gold and jewelled shrine was lit by hundreds of flickering candles. The Saint's presence formed the heart of a national pantheon. Into this Abbey, known to and venerated by all her

predecessors, processed Elizabeth II, surrounded by the full panoply of her
ancient state and massive Commonwealth. She moved through the soaring
aisle to kneel before Saint Edward's shrine.

The setting was indeed golden, though, not with candles so much as the
great electric lights required for the television broadcast. The building was
far from empty; it was packed with glittering greatness; the trumpets flour-
ished and the bows danced on a hundred violins; the organ growled its
punctuation and the choirs welcomed the tiny royal novice, as she walked
serenely to the altar between a phalanx of tall military body guards.

The words of the 122nd Psalm, sung at the start of every coronation since
1626, encouraged the procession on.

I was glad when they said unto me, Let us go into the house of the Lord. Our feet shall stand within thy gates, O Jerusalem . . . Peace be within thy walls, and prosperity within thy palaces.

The music, written by Hubert Parry, subsided slightly as the Queen reached the great crossing and, with a dramatic impact which would have moved Henry III, the trumpets introduced the welcoming shouts of the Westminster Scholars, who exclaim the traditional Latin greeting, '*Vivat Regina Elizabetha*'. These acclamations, or *Laudes* were introduced to the Saxon service by William the Conqueror for his Queen's coronation. In Norman times, this practice was the preserve of Aachen. Their use by William expressed a claim of independence from the Holy Roman Empire and were consequently deeply significant. Colin Borg was one of the Westminster scholars:

I think all of us were tremendously taken aback by how small she looked, how fragile. I don't think she is very tall anyway but I think it was perhaps the majesty of the whole of the Abbey, the seating going up in great tiers, the banners and flags and so on. But she looked almost lonely in the middle of this procession, surrounded by her courtiers and so on – it was a huge procession of course.

The Coronation service is divided simply into five sections; Recognition, Oath, Anointing, Investiture and Homage. Each is in balance with the rest. Without one, under the Laws of Saint Edward and in the spirit of Britain's constitution, there cannot be the other.

The five stages begin with the Recognition; here the Queen's election, legally performed at the Accession Council in February 1952, is affirmed by the people. The Archbishop is about to impart the holy sacrament of unction, so he needs to be absolutely sure that he has the right person. Historically, the Sovereign drew supreme power from the gift of unction; as God's anointed, no mortal could question his status. It was vital that the right person was anointed.

The Queen stood alone beside Saint Edward's Chair, while the Archbishop, flanked by the mediaeval Great Officers of State, went to the four Sides of the elevated Theatre and shouted:

Sirs, I here present unto you Queen Elizabeth, your undoubted Queen: wherefore all you that come this day to do your homage, are you willing to do the same?

From each direction of the compass rang out the reply, 'God save Queen Elizabeth!' The Scholars join in this shout too, theoretically to represent the masses outside the Abbey walls because, in the past, the doors were flung open at this stage of the ceremony, to enable the crowds to join in. After each reply the trumpets echoed the crowd's enthusiasm and the Queen curtsied a deep obeisance to her people, before turning South, West and North. Once he is satisfied by the shouts of approval, the Archbishop still needs to be sure that the new monarch will not run riot under the protection which the unction offers.

Thus comes the second stage of the inauguration, the Oath. Few parts of the ceremony have undergone so much change since Saint Dunstan drafted

The most private part of the Coronation ritual is the anointing. A canopy was placed over the Queen and film and television cameras were switched off.

King Edgar's. Almost every monarch has entered into prolonged debate over the wording. It has been the bartering point for centuries. It became a three-way struggle between Monarch, Parliament and Church. Each Coronation Oath, since the earliest times, gives a clue to the balance of power which existed at the time. In 1953 there were huge discussions over the evolving nature of the Commonwealth and how this should be reflected in the wording. In January 1993, the coronation oath was in the news once more. The Archbishops of Canterbury and York felt there should be change; the Church should take a lower profile. What does that say of the balance of power in 1993?

The Archbishop asked the Queen, 'Madam, is Your Majesty willing to take the Oath,' and she replied, 'I am willing.'

Will you solemnly promise and swear to govern the Peoples of the United Kingdom, of Great Britain and Northern Ireland, Canada, Australia, New Zealand, the Union of South Africa, Pakistan and Ceylon, and of your Possessions and the Territories to any of them belonging or pertaining, according to their respective laws and customs?

I solemnly promise to do so.

The threefold oath goes on to cover the preservation of all extant laws and the maintenance of the established Church. It is confirmed by signature on the Coronation Roll. This document, kept in the Public Record Office, can be brought to the Sovereign's attention by Parliament, should she break her trust.

Before the inauguration proceeded further, the Moderator of the Church of Scotland presented a copy of the Holy Bible. It is the Church's opportunity to remind the monarch where to draw inspiration from, in the conduct of affairs. The Moderator used the succinct instruction:

Here is Wisdom; this is the royal Law; these are the lively Oracles of God.

At last the Archbishop is satisfied that he not only has the right Sovereign, properly elected and recognized, but also that she has contracted with her People to govern according to law. The service moves to the most venerable and holy part of the coronation, the Anointing. Lady Rayne was able to watch the sacred moment from where the Maids of Honour were standing.

There were so many vivid memories. The one that I found most moving was the scene when the Queen is anointed. She stands there, slightly apart from everyone else, with a very simple linen shift over her dress, unadorned, no crown, no jewels, nothing. She looked so slim and young and very vulnerable. It was the most solemn part of the ceremony.

The 'linen shift' Lady Rayne remembers is very significant. In England's early coronations, many of the Byzantine customs were adopted. When the time came for unction the Byzantine Emperors would discard all temporal glory and present themselves at the altar in the garb of a humble peasant. This plain linen garment, based on what the eastern peasants wore, is called the *Colobium Sindonis*. The atmosphere of the ceremony is made all the more ethereal by the wonderful setting by Handel of the Bible's reference to one of the first unctions: 'Zadok the Priest and Nathan the Prophet anointed Solomon king: and all the people rejoiced and said God save the king! May the king live for ever!'

During this, the Queen removed the Robe of State, her diadem, and Collar of the Garter. Over her magnificent coronation dress went the *Colobium Sindonis*, which made her look pure and ready for God's grace. Her predecessors were required to fall prostrate on the floor, to complete this act of humility. The Queen went and sat in Saint Edward's Chair, which contains Scotland's Stone of Destiny and was made for Edward I after a victorious campaign in the northern kingdom. Four Knights of the Garter brought a canopy of golden cloth to cover the Queen and further protect and sanctify the moment. The golden Ampulla, shaped like an eagle, and Anointing Spoon were brought from the altar. The eagle is one of the biblical beasts and was the messenger of the Gospel. As the unction sacramentally confers the sevenfold gifts of the Holy Spirit, it is brought to the Queen from the altar in the eagle. The cameras were turned away and many diverted their gaze as the Archbishop dipped his hands into the specially consecrated oil and placed a cross on the Sovereign's hands, breast and head.

And as Solomon was anointed King by Zadok the priest and Nathan the prophet, so be thou consecrated Queen over the Peoples.

The Queen is now ready to be given the insignia of her kingdom, so she is dressed in the other magnificent robes, which derive from Byzantine and Rome, before the Investiture begins. Each part of the regalia is symbolic. Of course no magical wisdom, power or virtue is conveyed in the investitures; both the People, on whose authority the Archbishop delivers the insignia, and the Queen, recognize what is meant by the symbolism. Dressed in the 'Supertunica', a cloth of gold coat, similar to the one worn by a Roman Consul, she receives Saint George's Spurs and the Jewelled Sword of State. The Sword is one of four at the ceremony. The other three

BELOW: *The Queen receives the Orb. Like other pieces of the regalia, its design dates back to Ancient Greece.*

are symbolic of the three divisions of power and are carried throughout the service by Peers. One of these, called Curtana, has a blunted end. According to legend, Oggiero the Dane was about to strike his enemy dead when the Angel of God knocked it from his hand, saying, 'Mercy is better than revenge.' Curtana was carried to remind the Queen of the mercy she should exercise in administering justice.

The new Commonwealth wanted to make a contribution to the ceremony. After much thought, the Armills or Bracelets of Sincerity and Truth were revived. Last used at the coronation of Edward VI in 1547, bracelets used to be attached to a neck stole. It was like wearing a straight jacket and reminded monarchs to constrain their actions. Doubtless they never forgot. The simple golden bracelets were given by Canada, South Africa, Australia, New Zealand, Pakistan, Ceylon and Southern Rhodesia. The prayer offered as the Archbishop fastened them to the Queen's wrists described them as 'pledges of that bond which unites you with your Peoples.'

The Mistress of the Robes and Lord Great Chamberlain helped the Queen into the Stole Royal, which is rather like the scarf a priest wears, and the Pallium, or Robe Royal. Both are made of a thick cloth of gold fabric and the Robe was first used by George IV in 1821.

When Edward the Confessor's body was exhumed for Translation by Thomas à Becket in 1163, the robes which surrounded his corpse were removed. Instead of using a rectanglar imperial robe of Byzantium, meant to represent the four corners of the world, at this point in the service, English Kings were vested in Edward's decaying but saintly robes. It is believed they lasted until the regalia were destroyed by the Parliamentarians in 1649. The symbols of royalty were dangerous to Cromwell's plans by their very existence. They were the ideal rallying point for King Charles and the royalists. Such was the power of the regalia's symbolic value. Parliament's agent, Henry Marten, was sent to make an inventory:

ABOVE: *The Queen was crowned with the St Edward's Crown which was specially remodelled for her.*

He (Marten) was an enemy also to the Kingly Office and all belonging thereunto, especially the Regalia, which he caused to be sold; for being authorized by the said Parliament . . . he forced open a great iron chest within the College of Westminster and thence took out the crowns, robes, sword and sceptre belonging anciently to Edward the Confessor, and used by all our Kings at their inaugurations; and, with a scorn greater than his lusts and the rest of his vices, he openly declared that there should be no further use of those toyes and trifles. And in the jolity of that humour he invested George Wither (an old Puritan satirist) in the royal habiliments: who being crown'd and royally array'd (as right well became him) did first march about the room with a stately garb, and afterwards with a thousand apish and ridiculous actions exposed those sacred ornaments to contempt and laughter.

Athenae Vol IV, p. 1238

Wearing her great and heavy robes, which weigh nearly 17lbs, the Queen relied on the Bishops of Durham, and Bath and Wells to help her move around. Seated back in the simple, gnarled wooden chair, the Orb was placed in her right hand. It represents the dominion of Christ over all creation. Roman Emperors were depicted symbolically with their foot on the orb and their hand guiding the tiller of the universe. Small orbs appear on both sceptres and on the top of all royal crowns. The ring is placed on the fourth finger of the right hand; it is known as the "Wedding ring of England" and signifies the monarch's marriage to the country.

Before the Sceptre of Kingly Power is delivered, a single glove is placed on the Queen's right hand. Its symbolic value comes from one of the many legends associated with Edward the Confessor, who is supposed to have had a dream, wherein he visited the Royal Treasury to investigate a great commotion. When he opened the door, he saw the figure of a black devil dancing menacingly on chests containing the Danegeld. The Danegeld was a deeply unpopular and punitive poll tax, introduced by the Danish Kings of England. Edward immediately revoked the tax, undertaking never to levy the like again. The glove reminds the Queen to exercise power with compassion and to be 'gentle in taxation'. This simple and evocative symbol may have encouraged the Queen to advise and warn her Prime Minister against the disastrous reintroduction of the poll tax in the 1980s.

BELOW: *The moment every Archbishop dreads: ensuring that the crown is placed on the Sovereign's head the right way round.*

After the two sceptres of power and mercy are delivered, all that remains is the crown. As the moment approached, things didn't go so well for Lady Glenconner, one of the Maids of Honour:

When the Queen was [about to be] crowned, we were standing. I was one of the girls at the back, very luckily, because I started to feel very faint. We'd been up very, very early and had been standing around. Luckily Black Rod, who was standing beside me, saw my sort of green face and put his arm across me, to sort of hold me back against the pillar. And the Queen also, I think, saw that I was not feeling very well, and signalled that I should go out. But I was determined to see her being crowned, and so I was all right in the end.

An extra witness arrived just in time for the crowning, as Lady Moira Campbell recalls:

The Royal Box was immediately above where we were standing, and I remember hearing a rustle and little whispers going on, which I then realized was the arrival of Prince Charles, which, certainly to us, was a complete surprise because I don't think there had been any formal warning that he was going to join in.

The great golden crown of Saint Edward, crafted by Robert Vyner in 1661 for the bewigged head of Charles II, is both enormous and looks almost identical front and back. The Archbishop checked for the little golden stars placed to mark the front. He lifted the crown from its cushion and held it high above the Queen's head; not because he had to but because this had been practised to ensure his cope slipped back and didn't spoil the camera's view of the moment of crowning. With theatrical delay and timing, Archbishop Fisher obeyed the instructions of the rubric and

reverently put it upon the Queen's head. At the sight whereof the people, with loud and repeated shouts, shall cry, GOD SAVE THE QUEEN. The Princes and Princesses, the Peers and Peeresses shall put on their coronets and caps . . . and the trumpets shall sound, and by a signal given, the great guns at the Tower shall be shot off.

That signal was Charles Vincent-Smith's responsibility. He sat in Whitehall with a radio to the Tower guns in one hand and a telephone to his observer in the other.

I believe he [the observer] was lying on his tummy with a direct view down over the throne, where he could actually see the moment that the Crown was brought down on Her Majesty's head. He started the countdown to me on the private line and I repeated this by radio to the guns.

Then the horrible suspense, wondering whether your message had got through or not Then I heard the gun . . . go off and I got a report back from the other batteries that [all the] guns had been fired and the job was done.

Fully robed, recognized, obligated, anointed and invested, the crowned Queen was helped from the historic wooden chair to the Theatre. In the great crossing envisaged by Henry III, she negotiated a platform of five steps to the Chair of Estate, which had stood empty, waiting for its occupant, throughout the service. Gathered around the seat were all the mediaeval

Great Officers of State. While these officers no longer hold any power, they still perform their feudal duties on behalf of the people. It is their duty to ceremonially give the kingdom to the Queen by lifting her into the Chair of Estate. The Bishops helped her up the steps as she concentrated on keeping the crown steady. They helped her turn by pulling the heavy golden robe round. Then, like a balletic rugby scrum, all the coroneted and crimson-clad Great Officers leaned in and, with the Bishops, guided the Queen into the throne. Thus she took possession of her kingdom.

In the fifth and final part of the inauguration, the Queen gets her reward for all the obligations and responsibilities she has undertaken. As she sits 'enthroned' she receives the Homage of her Peers. The official artist, Terence Cuneo, chose this moment for his painting.

I thought it was the best comprehensive moment of the whole ceremony. The Queen was in an ideal position and the people coming up to pay homage. The Duke of Edinburgh first (after the Bishops) and the Royal Dukes.

His massive canvas demonstrates the success of his position and vision. At the Queen's feet kneels her consort in mediaeval humility, as he pledges his life to her service.

I, Philip, Duke of Edinburgh, do become your liege man of life and limb, and of earthly worship; and faith and truth I will bear unto you, to live and die, against all manner of folks. So help me God.

ABOVE: *Terence Cuneo's vast canvas captures one of the most moving moments of the Coronation as the Duke of Edinburgh pays homage.*

It was certainly one of the most moving moments. A 31-year-old husband dedicating his support to his 27-year-old wife and Sovereign, while his hands were clasped within hers. As he stood, he touched her Crown and kissed her left cheek gently, being careful not to upset the heavy burden she was balancing.

Traditionally, while all the Peers did their fealty, largesse was thrown around the congregation. Luckily this practice has ceased. In its place, the Royal Mint struck a coronation medal which was widely circulated amongst the participants.

Because all coronations took place within the Roman Catholic Mass, since the Reformation they have been held within a service of Holy Communion. The Queen and Duke knelt together to take bread and wine. The Queen took off her Crown and it was handed to Sir George Bellew.

When I had the crown on my knee, holding it with two hands, it was there, perched in front of me, within twelve inches, for the space of nearly a quarter of an hour. So I had plenty of time to contemplate it.

First of all, I contemplated its beautiful jewels, its mass of gold, which explained why it weighed so much, but I also had time to contemplate the romantic side of this enormously valuable object which represented so much. And I thought of the number of people who had had it on their heads, had been Sovereigns of England.

The music had been an integral part of the Coronation's atmosphere. William Walton, the composer, went to town with the *Te Deum* which concluded the Coronation ceremony. It was alive with every sound and instrument available in the Abbey. As the choirs sang, the Queen was taken to Saint Edward's shrine for her private prayers and to remove all the golden robes. The last words of the *Te Deum* must have been keenly contemplated by the new Queen. 'O Lord, in thee have I trusted: let me never be confounded.' The recess was also an opportunity to relax. For Lady Glenconner, it was a chance to recover from the faint she had felt earlier on.

Well, the Archbishop was wonderful because, when we eventually got behind the Rood Screen with the Queen, he produced a bottle of brandy from out of his robes, and said to me, I think you probably need something to revive you. And so I had a swig and then all the other ladies said, I think we'd like one too, and I think even the Queen may have had a drop. Anyway, we all felt frightfully jolly when we eventually came back, with the trumpets sounding, and [processed] off down the Abbey.

The Queen and the Maids of Honour leave the Abbey. Like every other stage of the service, this one had been carefully rehearsed (see page 114).

Lady Rosemary Muir remembers a small accident during the recess.

My Mother said, well, in case you feel faint, you had better take one of these, and produced a little smelling salt. I just managed to pop it into the palm of my hand, in my glove. And, during the Recess, the Archbishop of Canterbury shook hands with us and, I'm afraid, broke this, which produced an incredible smell of ammonia throughout the room we were in. Nobody could quite understand where it was coming from but it had a sort of refreshing effect on everybody.

The Queen put on the Imperial State Crown and the Purple Robe of Estate, took up the Sceptre with the Cross and Orb and then processed away from Saint Edward's golden glow to the world that waited outside. Set in the diamond cross at the top of her crown sparkled the small sapphire reputed to have been taken from Saint Edward's finger, possibly by Thomas à Becket, in 1163.

By the time the Queen came to travel back to Buckingham Palace, it was afternoon and Commander Eric Verge was tired and soaking wet. He had been chosen to carry the Queen's Colour for Plymouth Command and had been in position outside the Admiralty since a quarter-to-eight that morning. His wife sat opposite in a stand with a friend and two thermos flasks of coffee, but the First Sea Lord had forbidden Colour Officers to eat on parade, so Commander Verge had to go without food or drink for more than nine hours:

The Royal Army Service Corps came along with bag meals for the sailors and when they got to our position, I had a young petty officer on either side, and the one on my right-hand side was given a bag meal, and of course passing the Colour they said 'Eyes left!' and saluted 'Eyes front!' and then gave a bag to the chap on the left and went on. And there was this dear old Cockney lady in the back, and she shouted out, 'Oi! What about 'im with the flag? Where's 'is dinner?'

RIGHT: *The Queen did not leave the Abbey until the afternoon. The crowds lining the processional route filled in the time listening to broadcasts of the service.*

I remember someone in the afternoon crept up behind me and slid their hand over my shoulder and popped a boiled sweet into my mouth. It was the only thing I had all day and it was contrary to rules and regulations but I enjoyed it.

William Davies recalls that the planners had taken account of the street-liners' other needs:

In the Navy the loos are called the 'heads'. We'd been trained during our time in Chatham Barracks that on the order 'Operation heads!', each of us grounded our rifle, stepped back and doubled away into the building behind us, which I believe was the Ministry of Defence. Every fourth man did this. When the man returned back to his position, the next man went, and so on and so on, right down the line. Not another word was spoken, not another order given. Just 'Operation heads!', fourth man away, and that was it.

The sailors like William Davies suffered more from the effects of the rain than the other street-liners:

In those days, the sailor's white hat was a white fabric which you had to blanco with white Blanco to keep up its whiteness. Now this was a special occasion, so all us clever sailor boys got some Meltonian shoe cream and we polished our caps to a very fine finish, which, of course, meant using an excessive amount of Blanco. So on the day we're there and eventually down our faces, into our eyes, comes the white Blanco. Now we're stood at attention with a rifle. I could have put my hand up, got my handkerchief and wiped my brow. Who would have noticed such a little movement? Who would have cared? But no. The naval discipline was we had to stay as we were. So a very kind St John's ambulance person came behind us and, where they saw it was troubling us, got a big wad of cotton wool and mopped our brows for us.

When Davies finally saw the Queen, his heart swelled with pride:

ABOVE: *The Gold State Coach travels slowly, at walking pace. This allowed the crowds a good view of their newly crowned Queen.*

LEFT: *By travelling in the Gold State Coach, the Queen continued a long-standing tradition. It has been used at every coronation since 1831.*

Well, when the procession reached me, I was very emotional about this, very proud. Because after all, I am British, in spite of being Welsh – we are British – and it was such a thrill, a thrill of pride to be taking part in this momentous moment in history. When you think about it, I'll never see another one at my age. I was very proud, very proud indeed.

Maureen Raper was also moved:

The most memorable and most exciting experience I'll ever recall was when she passed in her coach. She looked so beautiful, so delicate. She was tiny and she had a special smile. The smile seemed to radiate warmth and a sort of new beginning for everyone.

And as she passed the sun came out and there was a glint of silver light which seemed to go through the coach, creating a kaleidoscope of colour. She smiled and waved. It was almost as if she was smiling and waving directly at us, as if to say, 'Well, enjoy your special day as much as I'm enjoying mine.'

At least one member of the crowd standing next to Maureen Raper got quite carried away:

After the Queen had gone past there was a very overweight lady that had been standing next to us for a long time. She had got bored with waiting and just really was wanting the Queen to pass. So in her boredom she just ate one bread bun after the other. But when the Queen passed, she jumped for joy and joined in with the enthusiasm and cheered 'Hooray! God save the Queen! Hip-hip hooray!' And her teeth fell out into the gutter and everyone looked, wondering if they would be trodden on. But she said, 'Oh, blow the teeth. I don't care. Just hooray for Her Majesty!' And the teeth still stayed in the gutter.

Outside London, the nation had watched the processions and the Abbey service on television: a new and unforgettable experience for many people.

RIGHT: *Troops from all over the Commonwealth came to London to join in the celebrations.*

In the afternoon, villages and towns had prepared their own celebrations, although many, like the Coronation Sports in Melbourn, Cambridgeshire, had to be postponed because of the rain. Nothing, however, could dampen the spirits of Jackie Parry and her family in Cardiff, Wales. Her mother organized raffles to pay for a street party, and each Saturday Jackie and her friend Gloria collected sixpence from every house in the road for the tickets.

The morning of the Coronation it absolutely poured down, absolutely. So, of course, we were all disappointed, especially the kids. We didn't know whether the party was going to go ahead or no. So we waited. One of the neighbours had a television. So we watched the Coronation on this little black-and-white screen. The room was full, packed out. There were even children out on the window sills, looking through, trying to catch a glimpse of the Queen.

Finally, the rain stopped. Trestle tables covered with freshly-ironed bed sheets were laid out in the street. Mountains of jelly and custard were produced from every kitchen and the party began:

We had a piano. So my Dad and one or two of the men brought the piano from out of the house, put it in front of the house, and took the front off the piano so you could hear it. He started playing. He played lovely – he could play anything actually. So he played the piano and people started singing.

All the kids dressed up. I was Bo Peep, one of my brothers was a cowboy and the other one was a painter and decorator, and all his paints were red, white and blue.

There was a chap playing the accordion, and then our friendly coal man came along with the coal lorry which was all spruced up, all clean. My grandfather stood up there and he started playing the spoons. My Nana sang. Everyone sang. It was great.

Back in London, an exhausted Paul Scott was travelling home on the Underground to Fulham with some fellow members of the Coronation choir:

The Queen Mother rode in the Irish State Coach. Some carriages had to be borrowed from a film studio for the procession.

We four lads were sitting on the train, and, frankly, we were emotionally and physically knackered. It's the only word for it. A little old man was sitting opposite us and we had, of course, our robes and we had our scores with us. And he suddenly looked over at us, and he said, "'Ere, have you blokes been singing?" And we said we had. And he said, "What a funny day to hold a wedding, don't you know there's been a crowning on? You poor little buggers, you've missed one of the best days of your lives."

Outside Buckingham Palace, there was no holding the crowds once the procession was over. They surged forward shouting, 'We want the Queen!'

At twenty-to-six she appeared on the Palace balcony. A huge shout went up. One which, according to an onlooker, 'must have been heard from Hyde Park to the Horse Guards.' All eyes turned to see her from the rain-swept street. To Jane Rayne it was an unforgettable moment:

Standing on that balcony and looking right down the Mall, as far as you could see, there were just, well, thousands, maybe millions of people . . . They just stretched for ever, right into the distance. Pouring rain again, cheers, and absolutely so moving.

Few looked up in time to catch the first wing of RAF Meteors as they roared above the Mall in a salute modified by the poor weather. Within moments, the seven wings of twenty-four aircraft had disappeared over the high roof of the Palace and the crowd returned its adoring gaze to the

DAYS OF MAJESTY • 139

balcony. As night fell, there was dancing again in the streets of London. The congas were slower, the steps of the exhausted revellers less sure, but no one wanted the fairy tale to end. The soldiers had returned to their barracks, tents and underground shelters. The police were patrolling the streets, but they had little to do. Later, illuminations would light up the lowering sky and fireworks would spurt joyful patterns over the waters of the River Thames.

But first the nation paused to listen to the words of the Prime Minister, Sir Winston Churchill. It was a poignant moment. The great leader was old and the Queen he vowed to serve was young. The voice which had inspired the people of Britain in war spoke simply on this day of hope and peace:

We have had a day which the oldest are proud to have lived to see and which the youngest will remember all their lives. It is my duty and honour to lead you to its culmination.

Then it was the Queen's turn. She, too, chose simple words to bring to an end her greatest day of majesty:

Throughout this memorable day I have been uplifted and sustained by the knowledge that your thoughts and prayers were with me. I have been aware all the time that my peoples, spread far and wide throughout every continent and ocean in the world were united to support me in the task to which I have now been dedicated with such solemnity.

The ceremonies you have seen today are ancient and some of their origins are veiled in the mists of the past. But their spirit and their meaning shine through the ages, never perhaps, more brightly than now.

I have in sincerity pledged myself to your service, as so many of you are pledged to mine. Throughout all my life and with all my heart I shall strive to be worthy of your trust.

LEFT: *Another of Cecil Beaton's Coronation portraits. The Duke of Edinburgh is wearing the uniform of an Admiral of the Fleet.*

INDEX

PICTURE
ACKNOWLEDGMENTS

The publishers wish to thank the following photographers for taking pictures specially for this book: Shelley Klein for the photographs on pages 32, 33 (TR), 87, 102; Derrick Witty, page 72; Michael Harvey, page 35; Roy McAdam of the Norman Mays Studio, Malvern, page 43; Pat Dyos, pages 31, 94 (BL), 95, 96, 97 (both), 99; Brian Walker, page 100; Jayne Fincher, page 108.

The publishers would also like to thank the following sources: Tim Graham: 5, 45, 56 (both), 57, 84, 92, 93, 94 (TR), 107; Cecil Beaton/Camera Press: 6, 140; Woodmansterne: half-title, 8, 9, 52, 54 (both), 111, 121, 131, 136 (both), 137, 138, 141; Hulton-Deutsch Collection: frontispiece, 10, 12, 14, 15, 18, 25, 39, 86, 116, 117, 119, 125, 133 Evening Standard/Solo: 11 (BR); By Courtesy of the Dean and Chapter of Westminster: 11 (TL), 13; The Royal Collection 1993 © Her Majesty Queen Elizabeth II: 17, 49, 51, 69, 81, 90 (B), 91, 132; Tony Stone Worldwide: 19; Syndication International: 20, 89, 103, 105; Popperfoto: 22, 23, 24, 26, 38, 53, 109, 115, 120, 123, 127, 128, 129, 134, 135, 139; Yorkshire Television Copyright Pictures: 27 (both), 31, 33 (ML & BL), 46 (both), 94 (BL), 95, 96, 97 (both), 101 (both); Central Office of Information: 28; © 1993 Comstock/Julian Nieman/SGC: 29; Helen Hill: 30; Michael O'Mara Books Ltd: 32, 33 (TR), 87, 100, 102; Trustees of the Weston Park Foundation/The Bridgeman Art Library, London: 34 (TL); Lord Weatherill: 34 (BR); Museum Casts International photograph © Michael O'Mara Books Ltd: 35; Michael Holford/British Library: 36; Herald & Evening Times, Glasgow: 37; Tate Gallery, London: 41; Madresfield Estate: 43; Chester Cathedral Shop Ltd: 47; Guildhall Library, Corporation of London/The Bridgeman Art Library, London: 48; Chris Walton, by Courtesy of The Worshipful Company of Goldsmiths: 55; By Courtesy of the National Portrait Gallery, London: 58; By Courtesy of the Commissioners of the Royal Hospital Chelsea: 59; Press Association: 60; Collections/Brian Shuel: 61; Collections/Roger Scruton: 62, 64, 65; Public Relations (Army) London District: 63, 70, 71, 88; Courtesy of the Director, National Army Museum London: 67; British Library, London/The Bridgeman Art Library, London: 68, 90 (TL); By courtesy of His Grace the Duke of Wellington: 72; David Levenson/Colorific!: 73; Swan-Upping (1915–19) Stanley Spencer. © Estate of Stanley Spencer 1993. All rights reserved DACS. Tate Gallery, London/The Bridgeman Art Library, London: 75; Patrick Ward/Colorific!: 76, 77, 78, 82, 83; Norman Parkinson Ltd: 79; S & G Press Agency: 85; Sir Geoffrey Keynes Collection, Cambridgeshire/The Bridgeman Art Library, London: 98; Society of Antiquaries of London: 99; Granite Film & Television Productions Ltd: 108; Private Collection: 110, 114; Royal School of Needlework: 113

(BL – below left; BR – below right; B – below; TL – top left; TR – top right; ML – middle left)